FROST CUTLERY
History & Tribute

Scott Cuffe

First Edition

OZARK SMALL PRESS
FORSYTH, MISSOURI

OZARK SMALL PRESS

www.ozarksmallpress.com

Contents

FOREWARD 9

PREFACE 13

CHAPTER 1
LUNCH-BUCKET BEGINNINGS 17

CHAPTER 2
INTERVIEWS 21

    JAMES A. "JIM" FROST 24
    Founder, President and Chief Executive Officer

    MARGARET FROST 47
    Mother of Jim Frost

    STEPHEN FROST 51
    Son and Chief Operating Officer

    STEFANIE FROST-DURHAM 55
    Daughter and Executive Director

    JEFF DANIEL 60
    Senior Vice President

    ROBERT SIMPSON 69
    Former Salesman and Oldest Customer

    KEVIN PIPES 71
    Owner, Smoky Mountain Knife Works

    SCOTT COMBS 73
    Purchasing Agent

    JERRY LAWHORN 77
    Retail Showroom Manager (Retired)

    BOB JOHNSTON 79
    Phone Sales/Personnel/Warehouse Manager

    STACY COMBS 86
    Combs Customs Knife Maker

    LEE ROBERTSON 88
    Frost Falcons Softball/Assistant

    RHONDA BOONE 89
    Former Chief Executive Assistant

JAN WATSON 91
Information-Technology Director

MIKE SARRATORE 93
Corporate Account Salesman

TAMI WORLEN 99
Art Director

MICHAEL "SHORTY" SHERILL 102
Customizing Shop Supervisor

GEORGE AMES 104
Corporate Accounts Manager

PATRICK SHIPLEY 105
Assistant Corporate Accounts Manager,
Marketing Coordinator, EDI Coordinator

JAY HAGGARD 107
Corporate Sales/Softball Coordinator

PHIL MARTIN 109
Owner, Blue Ridge Knives

CHAPTER 3

THE CABLE SHOW 111

TERRY DUNCAN 113
Cable Show/Product Sales Manager

TOM O'DELL 117
Cable Show Host/Salesman

SHEILA TRAVIS 121
Cable Show Producer/Host

TODD BOONE 123
Cable Show Host/Salesman

CHAPTER 4

THE FROST FALCONS
Building Character One Pitch at a Time 134

APPENDIX 147

LEXICON 148

BRAND & TRADE NAMES 151

LETTERS & AWARDS 152

AFTERWARD 162

A NOTE FROM THE AUTHOR 164

FOREWARD

ONCE UPON A TIME, *a long time ago, in a land far, far away* . . . These are the familiar words we all expect to read at the beginning of a fairy tale.

But even though Jim Frost's story began once upon a time, a long time ago, in a land that may indeed be far, far away from you, dear reader, his is no fairy tale.

I have been fortunate to know and work for Mr. Frost for more than thirty years and this book is an accurate history of and tribute to a man I admire and respect. In the pages that follow you will experience the real-life triumph of a man who, beginning at a chemical plant over forty years ago as a modest, everyday shift worker, turned his hobby of collecting and trading knives into a multi-million dollar family business. As you read, not only will you share in the vision of a simple, hardworking laborer who became a sophisticated businessman and successful entrepreneur, you will also feel Jim's heartfelt compassion and desire to give back for the betterment of his community.

You will also taste Jim's passion for women's fastpitch softball and see how he has used his love of the sport to forever change the lives of countless young athletes. Leveraging his success in the cutlery business as well as a keen sense of philanthropy and leadership, Jim became a pioneer of the exciting game in Tennessee. Along the way he has been a tireless coach, advocate and promoter of women's fastpitch softball, and his famous motivational speeches echo across the hallowed diamonds and in the shadowed dugouts of softball fields throughout the Volunteer State. "Those who seek, listen, learn and utilize the intelligence of others are the wisest people in the world" are the words of wisdom that Jim has shared with thousands of student athletes throughout Tennessee and across the nation. The resounding message he conveys is that you are given just one life to live and what you choose to do with it is up to you. Some may choose to waste it away, but many will choose to follow their dreams and ambitions.

The inspirational story you will read in the pages that follow is no flight of fiction. Instead, it is the real-life tale of how dreams really can come true. Jim Frost is living his American dream. With perhaps the best chapter of his life yet to be written, he continues to help others achieve their own dreams through his generosity and also through his dedication to the youth of his community.

This "History & Tribute" will end with a final chapter written, and for you a final word read, but I promise this is truly not the end. Lives will continue to be impacted by Mr. Frost's generosity whether from past, present or future gifting. I know this as fact by hearing Mr. Frost's desire to fully fund a foundation that will hopefully carry on long after each of us. Life on earth is very short, but how you choose to live it, is your decision. I challenge you to seek Christ first, follow your heart and dreams, and may your ambitions be fulfilled. My family and I have truly been blessed and inspired by Mr. Frost's kindness and generosity. I am proud to call him my boss but I am honored more to call him my friend.

May you, dear reader, be inspired and blessed so that you can be an inspiration and a blessing to others as well.

JEFF DANIEL
SENIOR VICE PRESIDENT
FROST CUTLERY COMPANY

PREFACE

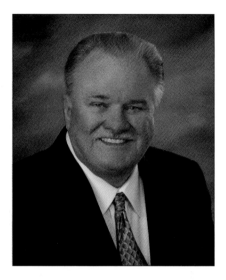

I OFTEN HEAR people talking about the American Dream. Some are chasing it, but I am blessed to be living it.

In part, I credit my very good fortune to one of the key philosophies I adhere to, both in life and in business:

"Those who make it a habit to seek, listen, and learn from the intelligence of others are the smartest people in the world."

I do my best every day to be just such a person. That's why I have made it a habit to surround myself with outstanding individuals like Jeff Daniel, who is Vice President of my company, Frost Cutlery.

I have also found there are no better people in the world than those who are involved in knives and knife collecting, and over the years I have made many wonderful friends in the business. As I think back on some of the more memorable trades I have made, I recall one in particular. I was at a trade show when I noticed a fella — I would later learn that his name was R. W. "Red" Tays — showing some nice German knives on his display table. I walked over, pointed to the knives and asked, "How much do you want for those?"

"Twenty-eight dollars," he replied.

"Twenty-eight dollars? How many do you have?"

"I have 100," he said, and — thinking I would make a killing on them at that price — I quickly replied, "I'll take all of them."

Red just smiled at me and said, "They're all yours."

Now Red was older than me and much wiser, and that trade proved it, because a few years later he told me that he had started out offering those knives for $18 each, but no one would buy them. Instead of slashing the price in hopes of attracting a buyer, he raised it to $20, then to $22 and again to $24, and still nobody would buy them. Refusing to give in, Red raised the price one more time. "I went to $28," he explained, "and when you came along I finally figured out what those knives were worth."

Red and I went on to be life-long friends, and for years I have laughed about that first trade with Red and the lesson I learned from it. Many times I've been beaten in a trade, but I have learned a valuable lesson from each and every one. Most important, I've learned that that is what you do in this world: You learn from your mistakes and in the end you benefit.

JAMES A. "JIM" FROST
FOUNDER AND CEO
FROST CUTLERY COMPANY

CHAPTER 1

Lunch-Bucket Beginnings

I T ALL BEGAN in 1969, more than four decades ago, when James A. "Jim" Frost sold a pocketknife to one of his co-workers, who selected his purchase from a small inventory Jim carried to work in his lunch bucket. It was an inauspicious start for what would one day become one of the world's leading cutlery merchandisers and manufacturers, the Frost Cutlery Company LLC.

Back then, Jim worked the third shift at the Farmers Chemical fertilizer manufacturing plant in Chattanooga, Tennessee. A hardworking family man with an incurable passion for knives and for selling, Jim carried his wares to work in his lunch bucket and every day, he recalls, "At lunch and on my breaks, I'd sell pocketknives to my co-workers." It was the simplest business model imaginable and one that offered several key advantages, not the least of which was that after every sale, Jim's customers paid for their purchases and took delivery right on the spot.

Most importantly, it worked.

Before long, Jim's elegantly simple retail marketing and distribution program, combined with his natural salesmanship, proved so successful that his lunch bucket simply couldn't carry enough knives. In order to accommodate the rapid growth of his business, Jim was forced to move the budding young company's operations out of his lunch bucket and into the trunk of his car, a 1966 Mustang where the business continued to grow.

In no time at all, Jim was forced to move the company into his garage and then to add a building behind his house. The months flew by, sales continued to grow, and the next move was into an office space of a few hundred square feet. As the decades passed, this pattern of growing then moving continued until 2002 when, after outgrowing several increasingly larger office buildings, Jim built an impressive 100,000-square-foot headquarters and warehouse complex in Ooltewah, Tennessee, conveniently located right next to Interstate 75. Incredibly, the growth didn't stop there and just two years later, in 2004, Frost Cutlery added an additional 50,000 square feet to its Ooltewah facility. According to Jim, this is the final location for the home of Frost Cutlery Company. However, given the company's remarkable history of growth, who can say whether and when yet another expansion will be required?

Humble beginnings, one might say. You certainly can't start any more humbly than by selling pocketknives from your lunch bucket at work. But a mighty oak begins as a tiny seed, and by taking a few knives that he bought and resold for a small profit, then continually planting those profits back into more and more inventory, Jim was taking the first steps on what would prove a most remarkable journey. This simple yet effective strategy enabled his company to grow and expand beyond his wildest dreams and, some thirty-nine years later, made Jim Frost one of the greatest knife sellers in the world.

Before he started Frost Cutlery, Jim had been working anywhere from fifty to eighty hours a week at his job at Farmers Chemical. His strong work ethic enabled him to earn a good living and provided a comfortable life for his family. But his real passion was in sales, in the meeting of people directly, speaking to an individual and getting to know them. Giving a friendly smile with a firm handshake plus pleasant conversation and, above all, treating the customer with courtesy and respect, honoring his word, and standing up for his products and their quality—these were Jim's stock in trade and the enduring keys to his success.

Today, Jim maintains the straightforward, hardworking, pay-as-you-go business philosophy that he started with so long ago and which has since served him in such good stead. He is especially proud of the fact that his company has always paid cash for its inventory, a practice that has consistently enabled the company to pay the lowest prices possible and sell its knives for a profit. As a result, Frost Cutlery strives to remain debt free to its vendors for inventories and supplies.

Throughout the years, despite a hectic work schedule and the growing demands of his business, Jim always found time to watch his two children practice and participate in school sports. As a result, he developed a strong passion for softball and has participated in all aspects of the game, from coaching, sponsoring teams and donating millions of dollars. Over the years Chattanooga became a household name in the world of women's fastpitch softball at the collegiate level, as well as to the US Olympic teams through some of Jim's endeavors.

Jim encourages higher education scholarships for the young women who have played on the community's many ball fields, including the one at the state-of-art Jim Frost Stadium in Chattanooga, Tennessee. Ralph Weekly, of the University of Tennessee in Knoxville, and Mike Candrea, of the University of Arizona considers Jim a pioneer in women's fastpitch softball. Both Weekly and Candrea have won gold medals for coaching the American Team in the Olympic sport of women's fastpitch softball.

In the 1970s, Jim enjoyed a brief but rewarding partnership with Jim Parker, selling under the name Parker-Frost Knives. In the 1980s Frost acquired an ownership interest in one of the greatest knife trademarks and companies of all time, the Hen & Rooster Knife Company of Solingen, Germany. Today, he is the sole owner of the Hen & Rooster brand in the United States. Indeed, over the last thirty-nine years, Jim has both created and acquired many trademarks and knife brands. In addition to Hen & Rooster, he owns many other German knife lines and deals with vendors in many nations in order to secure the knife products for sale through his Frost Cutlery Company.

Besides creating trademarks and brands, Jim personally designed countless numbers of knives and is directly involved in purchasing the knives his company sells. He is very active in all functions of the business and even though he has an executive office he also keeps a desk on the warehouse floor. Jim constantly roams throughout the complex, helping out wherever and whenever he is needed and overseeing day-to-day operations, including production of Frost

2011: Frost Cutlery's headquarters in Ooltewah, Tennessee.

Cutlery's own cable television show, *Cutlery Corner Network*.

Jim is thankful for his employees, many of whom have worked with him for decades. A prime example is Jeff Daniel, Senior Vice President and one of the people who Jim speaks of most highly. Jeff started at Frost Cutlery more than thirty-four years ago when he was just fourteen years old and lived right across the street from Jim.

Naturally, Jim is especially grateful for his family, and whenever he talks about his son, Stephen, and his daughter, Stefanie, his great love and affection for them is plain to see. He is proud that they are following in their father's footsteps, both in the business, where Stephen is now Chief Operations Officer and Stefanie plays an important role in the day-to-day operations of the company, and in their generosity to those within the community who are in need. It is worth noting that whenever Jim talked about his children for this book his eyes often brimmed with shining tears of pride and joy.

In writing this book, it was the author's privilege and great good fortune to speak with the many wonderful people associated with Jim Frost and the Frost Cutlery Company. Within the pages of this book they tell, in their own words, of their own history and friendship with Jim, about their relationship with Frost Cutlery and their community, and about how one remarkable man was able to realize the American Dream from humble lunch-bucket beginnings.

CHAPTER 2

Interviews

URING MY TRIP to the Frost Cutlery offices and warehouse in Ooltewah, Tennessee I was privileged to talk to more than twenty Frost Cutlery employees about their favorite Jim Frost story and their favorite Frost Cutlery story. Along the way, whenever the opportunity showed itself, I asked questions about their fellow employees and even technical questions about knives and the knife world. To say that I was flabbergasted at how pleasant my interviewees were is the understatement of the year.

I was struck with many recurring themes during these interviews with the family, friends, and employees of Frost Cutlery. For instance, how they all seemed to be wonderful people in their own right, how they wanted to make Mr. Frost happy and proud of them, and how much they cherished their life and career with Frost Cutlery. And the characters that I met on this journey were colorful, to say the least; Jim Frost's mother, Margaret Frost, is truly one of the great ladies and characters of all time. Mr. Frost got his sense of humor, his dedication to his fellow man and his hard work ethic from his mother, of this I am sure. Another employee, Bob Johnston kept me in stitches with stories about Jim Frost and his Tennessee colloquialisms.

Stacy Combs and his brother Scott described their wonderful lives with Frost Cutlery and Mr. Frost himself. Likewise, I met many professional staffers such as Tami Worlen, Rhonda Boone and Jan Watson; as well as many others from Frost Cutlery's energetic sales staff, such as Jerry Lawhorn, Mike Sarratore, and George Ames. Others such as Lee Robertson and Jay Haggard described the Frost Cutlery commitment to the sport of softball, not only in the Chattanooga, Tennessee, area, but in every corner of this country where softball is played.

Jim Frost (shown here standing center back row, second from left) gathers for a group photo with just some of the first shift associates in the Frost Cutlery warehouse.

During a break between interviews with Frost Cutlery staff, Vice President Jeff Daniel and I spoke about the amazing softball odyssey of Jim Frost. While we were talking, Jeff put in a call to Ralph Weakly, an Olympic coach and co-head coach[1] of the University of Tennessee Lady Vols women's fastpitch softball team. When we called, Coach Weakly was at the Women's College World Series recruiting for his University and potential Olympic Teams. He was there along with legendary Olympic Coach Mike Candrea, Head Coach of the University of Arizona Wildcats women's fastpitch softball team, who like Weakly was also recruiting. Not only did both of these men take time out of their busy schedule to speak with me about Jim Frost, they were excited and glad to do it. In fact, Coach Weakly ended up calling Jeff's cell phone four separate times that day to provide additional material for this book.

During one of those calls Coach Weakly told me, "All of the growth in Tennessee softball is attributable to Jim Frost.

"He is a very good coach," Weakly said. "He is always a gentleman.

---

1   Coach Weakly shares head coach responsibilities at UT with his wife, Karen Weakly.

This carries over to his business.

"I respect the man, I owe him a lot, and his legacy will be, as Jim always says, 'It's all about the kids.' Hundreds of kids have received scholarships because of his stadium."

Coach Weekly then handed his cell phone to Coach Candrea, who confirmed all that Coach Weekly had said, saying, "Jim Frost is the pioneer of women's fastpitch softball. We need more people like him."

Jeff and I were amazed at how these two great men would take the time to talk to us during their busiest time of the year, while scouting and giving out scholarships to their Universities. In itself we considered this to be a great tribute to Mr. Frost, even before they shared with us their praise and respect for Mr. Frost.

Each interview I conducted excited me more than the last. Before I knew it, fourteen hours went by the first day, and twenty-two hours passed by on the second day during my trip to Frost Cutlery in Ooltewah, Tennessee. Later, I conducted many telephone interviews with Frost Cutlery friends, family, employees and others. Here are their stories, in their own words, as they were told to me.

James A. "Jim" Frost

Founder, President and Chief Executive Officer

Tell us about yourself.

Well, there's not a whole lot to tell, really. I was born to Margaret and Austin Frost on the thirteenth of November 1941 in the shadow of Missionary Ridge in Chattanooga Tennessee, not far from where Interstate 24 cuts through the ridge today. I went to Red Bank High School on Dayton Boulevard and graduated in 1959. The old school is gone now, moved to a new location, but I played football there and I was all-state.

James A. Frost, 1959

What position did you play?

I was a split end, or what was referred to in those days as a lonesome end. I'd line up on the scrimmage line maybe twenty yards outside of the offensive tackle. I played both ways and I was a linebacker on defense. I liked playing split end best because I got to catch passes, but it didn't matter as long as I was on the field and in the game.

Do you have any brothers or sisters?

I have one brother, Ed. He is about five years younger than me. Growing up, we lived in a little four-room house and Ed and I shared a bedroom. It had twin beds in it and the room was so small that we only had about a foot between the two beds. When I got up in the morning, I had to walk sideways just to get out of the room.

What did your father do for a living?

My dad was a construction worker, so he was always on the move, following the construction trade. When I was a kid we moved all over the South and we lived a very nomadic lifestyle. I was a freshman in high school when we finally settled down.

Who did you get your work ethic from; your mom or your dad?

I think it came from my mom. My dad was gone a lot, working out of town, as I was growing up, and she was always there for me. My dad passed away but my mom is still alive and she does a lot of work with charities, which she loves to do.

Did you go to college?

No. I graduated from Red Bank High in 1959 and went right straight into the work force. After several years, I finally took a job at the Farmers Chemical Association plant in Chattanooga, Tennessee.

How long did you work at the Farmers Chemical plant, what did they make and what was your job?

Farmers Chemical made urea and ammonium nitrate, which are both key ingredients in fertilizer. I worked there from the late 1960s on into the mid 1970s. I started off as an ordinary shift worker, but by the time I quit in 1976 I was responsible for operating the control board for the equipment that combined anhydrous ammonia with concentrated nitric acid in order to produce ammonium nitrate.

Was it a big responsibility?

Yes, it was a huge responsibility; making ammonium nitrate is a hairy job. The control board was probably forty foot long, it had about a thousand things on it and I'd say there were about 200 different readings on it that you had to keep up with. You had to make sure every one of those readings was within certain parameters. And because ammonium nitrate is explosive, we had to shut down the equipment whenever we had a thunderstorm or a lightning storm. That could be a real nightmare.

Did you ever think that the knife business would impact your life the

way it has?

Well, I have been richly blessed to have a very successful business doing something that I really enjoy doing. But without question, the most important thing about Frost Cutlery is that I am blessed to have my son and daughter, both wonderful people, working with me in the business, as well as Jeff Daniel and several other key employees who have been with me for years and years. You cannot fail in life if you surround yourself with good people, and I have done that. The people around me make me a success.

Had you always been interested in knives?

I was interested in anything that I could sell. I always felt that I had a unique ability to communicate with people, so selling came easy to me. I used to sell jewelry out of my pocket. When I was about seventeen years old, I went down to Cordell, Georgia, bought a load of watermelons and brought them back to the local farmer's market and sold them. Years later, when the freeway came through town, I bought houses and tore them down and sold the bricks and lumber that I salvaged out of them. So I was always an entrepreneur looking for ways to make money and not afraid to work to get there. But I always really enjoyed selling or communicating with people.

It just happened that I fell into knives. At the same time I went into knives, I also had an opportunity to go into two other businesses that each became highly successful. I had three opportunities to choose from and I picked the one I was most comfortable with at the time, which was knives.

You mentioned buying watermelons in Cordell, Georgia, and then reselling them at the local farmer's market. We heard there is a pretty interesting story about that experience; would you like to share it with us?

Yeah, well as I said, in the summertime when school was out, one of the things I did to make some money was that I went with a friend of mine down to Cordell to get a load of watermelons and bring them back to sell at the farmer's market here in Chattanooga. The thing is, you had to stay in the market all night with them, nobody was going to protect them for you, and so somebody had to stay with them. So I was out there with my watermelons and a guy next to me was set up with his watermelons. I dozed off and when I woke up, it was about one o'clock in the morning and I saw the guy next to me sell a watermelon off of my truck, and then replace it with one off of his truck.

Why was he selling your watermelons and replacing them with his? Were your melons better than his?

Well his customer wanted a watermelon that he saw on my truck. You know how it is when you see the one you want. So the guy just came over and got my watermelon off the back of my truck, sold it to his customer like it was one of his own, and then replaced it with one of the watermelons from his own truck.

Now back then—this must have been about 1958—I think we paid fifty cents for each watermelon and we sold them at the farmers market for a dollar. So I went up to this guy, who was about thirty years old and probably outweighed me by a hundred pounds, and I said to him, "I want my money for my melon. I didn't say you could sell my melons."

The guy said, "Well, I replaced the melon," and I said, "I don't care; that was my watermelon you sold and I want my dollar."

Well, we proceeded to get into a fight over those watermelons and you know that guy just beat the snot out of me; I mean he just tore me up. In the end, after he beat me up pretty good and he was standing over me, I looked and said to him, "If you sell another one of my watermelons, you're going to have to beat me up again, because I want my dollar."

Did you get your dollar?

No, I never did get my dollar, but that guy never sold another one of my watermelons either. He didn't want to go to the trouble of beating me up again so he didn't sell any more of my watermelons. I guess he decided it just wasn't worth the effort.

When you first started selling knives from your lunch bucket to your coworkers at Farmers Chemical, did you know it would eventually allow you to quit your job?

No. When I first started selling knives, I was a shift worker at the plant, putting in anywhere from fifty to eighty hours per week with a lot of overtime. I worked there and sold my knives there until 1976. When I realized I was making more money selling knives than I was working my job at the plant that's when I finally I said, "Hey, it's time to leave."

Was this risky in your mind?

In my mind, it wasn't. I was confident enough in what I was doing to quit a very good job with a very good company so I could do what I wanted to do.

Where did you get your knives to resell in the lunch-bucket days?

I would buy knives at hardware stores and resell them. If I bought a knife for $5 and sold it for $5.50, I made fifty cents. I went for the small profit. I put my profits back into buying more inventory that I could sell, and I did this over and over again until I had enough money to go into business, a bigger business.

I also used to buy a lot of knives from a gentleman named James F. Parker, who was in the knife business at that time. I would buy knives from him at wholesale and sell them at a minimal profit. When I quit my job at the chemical plant in 1976, I was able to go into business with Parker because I had saved up my money by selling those knives for fifty cents profit apiece. By the time I left the chemical plant I had accumulated about $50,000 and that enabled me to go into business with Jim Parker.

Your partnership with Parker ended in 1978. Why the split?

It was a difference in our business philosophies. I'm not saying that mine was right or his was right or either one of us was wrong, but Jim was more of a person to work with banks to advance his business and I was more of a pay-as-you-go person. After we split up, Jim went on

Pictured from left to right: Jim Parker (Jim's former partner, 1976–78), knife collector Hubert Lawell, Jim's brother Ed Frost, and Jim Frost.

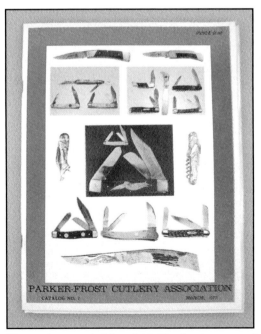

Shown above and at top right: The front cover and a spread from the Parker-Frost Cutlery Association Catalog No. 1, March 1977. Bottom right: *In the beginning . . .*

The trunk of a 1966 Ford Mustang was Jim Frost's first warehouse.

Jim Frost's home where he first started selling knives in his garage.

Office/storeroom addition to the back of the Frost's home.

and did well. It was nothing more than a difference in philosophies that caused us to separate. We were friends until he passed away in 2004. His successful business lives on today under the direction of his children, who have been and continue to be instrumental in the success of the Parker family business. I am still friends with his wife and son.

How did you come to purchase the Hen & Rooster brand?

I was in a friend's office, Howard Rabin, of Star Sales in Knoxville, Tennessee, and this was in the early 1980s. Howard said to me, "Jim, Hen & Rooster is going into receivership; were you aware of that?"

I told him, "I didn't know that; let's buy it!"

Howard said, "Do you think it is worth the money?" And I said, "Absolutely! Let's buy it now!" So he said to me, "I think it will take about $50,000.00," and I wrote him a check right there on the spot. We wired the money to Germany and we bought it out of receivership.

Later on, Howard sold his half of Hen & Rooster to me and I have been the sole owner since about 1986. Howard had no intentions of being long term; he was an older gentleman and he has long since passed away. Frost Cutlery now owns one of the finest, if not the finest, German cutlery trademarks in the world today.

Do you ever travel abroad to buy knives?

I have been to Spain, China and Japan buying knives. Jeff Daniel has been a few times to Germany, and Scott Combs has been to Germany, but I have never been there.

Is any country easier than another to negotiate with for your knife purchases?

They are all hard, none of them are easy. They are all very shrewd businessmen and they work very hard to make their profits, so it is all about negotiation. One of the most memorable negotiations I was involved with was in the mid eighties, when I went to Japan with a friend of mine named Doug. We were in a conference room with Doug and myself on one side of a large table, and on the other side sat the owner of the knife company, two accountants and more than thirty in-house sales executives—about forty people in total. It was a huge table, about eight feet wide, and every sales executive had his respective line of knives lying in front of him. I looked over the goods, priced about eight or ten items, and then didn't say a word as I waited for the sales executives to respond to my offers.

The company's financial officer's name was Mr. Osama. After his people countered with their pricing I looked at them as I got up from my chair. They were all looking at me as I walked to the end of the room, poured myself a cup of coffee, took a couple of sips and walked back to my chair. I sat my coffee down and looked at all of them. Then I slammed the table just as hard as I could and I looked at the owner and said, "You tell Mr. Osama that he needs to leave the room and sharpen his pencil or we won't buy anything today!"

They all got excited and started talking and eventually we got together and I bought over a million dollars worth of product that day. It was a memorable day for me. It was just so dramatic; they were all watching me, nobody was talking and I slammed that table hard. We sold more knives that year than we had prior.

How many knives have you designed? Do you have a favorite?

Thousands and thousands! I usually look at knives and put combinations together. Sometimes I will draw one out on paper. There are so many that I like. Steel Warrior, a line of Frost knives, has done really well, and Hen & Rooster is a great line. I would have to say that in value, Hen & Rooster is the best. It is just like kids, you have five kids, and how do you pick a favorite? You can't. In their own way, all the lines are really great, and they all have their finer points.

Frost Cutlery has had a long and very successful relationship with NASCAR legend Dale Earnhardt and his company, Dale Earnhardt, Inc. Can you share a little about your relationship with Dale?

Dale was not just Dale Earnhardt the business associate, he was my friend. Dale was always a big jokester, and so he was always messing with me, always cutting up and clowning around. For example, one time I drove over to Dale's house in North Carolina to see him, and when I got there he walked out the front door and said over his shoulder as he passed me by, "I've got to go out of town, and I'll see you in a week." He got in his car and drove out the gate before he turned around and came back, laughing at the look on my face.

Another time, I had just bought a brand new Jeep Cherokee and I drove it over to North Carolina to see Dale. Dale lived in a big log home on a large piece of rural property located not far from his racing shop. So I pulled up to his front porch in that new Jeep Cherokee and, Dale being a Chevrolet driver, he said to me, "What are you doing driving that piece of junk?"

I said, "That ain't junk, it's a good car," and Dale said, "Well, let me drive it and I'll show you around my place."

So we took off in my Cherokee for a tour of the Earnhardt homestead. There was a dirt and gravel road that went around the perimeter of the property, and it had a lot of potholes in it—big potholes. Now Dale wasn't known for driving slow—on or off the track—and so he was gunning my brand new Jeep Cherokee down that dirt road at a pretty good clip. Dale drove me all around his property and showed me his lake, his house and his chicken houses, and I swear to you that he did not miss even one of those potholes. I mean, he hit every one of them wide open.

When we finally got back to the house, Dale got out, handed the keys to me and said, "You might want to trade this thing; it feels to me like the undercarriage is a little bit loose."

I stood there with the keys in my hand, my mouth wide open and a big "what-did-you-just-do?" look on my face, and it wasn't too much later that I had to trade that Cherokee in. In fact, I traded it in on a brand new Chevrolet truck.

Besides being a great practical joker, Dale was a great family man, too. He and his wife, Teresa, were very close and he really relied on her for her advice. He involved her in everything. I remember that when I'd go over to see Dale about the knives we were creating, Teresa would help us with the art work and also with the color selections for the products and even for the packaging. Later, when I would come back with a big box full of production samples for Dale to look over and approve, if Teresa wasn't there he wouldn't even look at them until she could look at them with him. He'd be dying to see those knives but he would say "Let's wait for Teresa to get back first."

Teresa had a lot of good business sense and Dale was very appreciative of that. He was a hard nosed man's man but he was dependent on Teresa for a lot of solid advice because he knew she had his best interest at heart. We'd sit there together, the three of us, and go over all the knives, checking the position of Dale's signature and his likeness and a hundred other little details, just to make sure everything was just right. I remember thinking how much Dale liked for Teresa to be involved in what we were doing and I thought it was great.

What was it like when you heard about Earnhardt's accident at the 2001 Daytona 500?

It was devastating. To know the real Dale Earnhardt was like . . . he was an unbelievable person. He was the type of person that commands your respect, and he would give you his respect if he liked you. And if he liked you, you couldn't ask for a better friend.

Dale was also an honest and an honorable man. Together Dale and I did a huge amount of business over the years, selling cutlery products with his likeness and signature on them, and we did it all on the basis of a handshake agreement. In nearly twenty years of doing business with Dale he never had to call for a check. To this day, one of the things that I cherish as much as anything is that handshake agreement between two honorable men that, in this day and time, is just too hard to find.

Does that handshake with Earnhardt still stand?

It has for over twenty years. A few months after Dale died; some folks from DEI [Dale Earnhardt, Inc.] called and said they were looking for a copy of the contract between DEI and Frost Cutlery. They said, we've done millions of dollars in business with you and we don't have a contract. And I said well I've got that contract with me. And they said, well can we have it? I said, it's in my pocket—it's my hand

and it's stronger than anything that you could put on paper.

Is it true that your first million dollar seller was a two-knife Dale Earnhardt commemorative set?

It is and I was extremely proud of it because that was for Dale Earnhardt. I knew Dale would be really happy and for that reason I was glad. Dale Earnhardt was a man's man. When you were in his presence he commanded respect just by the aura around him. He was a man of real worth and value and it was my privilege and my honor to know him from about 1985 until he passed away.

Frost Cutlery is famous for its knife handles that are made out of a unique and beautiful laminated wood material called Frostwood. Where does Frostwood come from?

Years ago, I happened to be at a show in Atlanta and I saw a piece of laminated wood. Actually, it was on a gun stock. I said to myself that would look good on a knife. So I bought a block and turned it into what we then named Frostwood. I trademarked the name and since then we've sold millions of knives with Frostwood scales and handles.

To this day, people ask, "Where does Frostwood come from?" and "What is this? We've never seen anything like this before."

A customer in Scottsboro, Alabama, once asked me where Frostwood comes from and I jokingly answered, "This has been something we have been working on for years. We actually grow those trees in Brazil." Then I told him, "It takes twenty years for the Frostwood trees to reach the proper height and thickness so we can harvest them and bring them here to make knife handles."

I thought, gosh, nobody will ever believe this. But it wasn't too long afterwards that I got a call from California and some fellow asked me if he could talk me out of some of those trees that we were growing. I had to tell him the truth but I couldn't stop the rumors; it really went around the world. People were going crazy trying to figure out where those trees were being grown for us. It was hilarious.

Why do you conduct Rockwell Hardness Testing on some of your

company's knife blades?

In general it is believed that to get the sharpest, longest lasting edge on a knife blade the Rockwell Hardness should be around 58 on the scale, so we have our blades tested. They are tested with a diamond point press and the blades must test between a Rockwell Hardness of 56 to 58 to be acceptable for the Steel Warrior knife and Frost Family Series knives. We feel like this sets these knives apart from any regular knife. A lot of knives from other manufacturers come in with 440 [a number signifying a high grade stainless steel] stamped on their blades when they are really 420 or even lower. We want our knives to be exactly as advertised, or better.

How did the Frost Family line of knives get its start?

The way that line came about was that I had been doing some research about the history of my family and I discovered that there was actually a real crest, a true crest of the Frost family that had belonged to my family's European ancestors. So we kicked it around for awhile and finally decided it might be a good idea to start a line of knives to honor that family heritage. Each Frost Family line of knives is made with a particular knife handle material for just 365 days and then discontinued forever. The shield inlaid into the handle is a replica of the Frost family crest.

Why limit the production of these knives?

We limit them to make them more collectible, more special. For example, when I was with Parker-Frost Knives, we made hundreds of thousands of knives of each pattern. But certain patterns like the Little Bandit knives had small production runs. Today you can look high and low for a Parker-Frost Little Bandit and you probably won't find one. Where are they? They're scarce and because of that scarcity they are prized by collectors. I go to a lot of knife shows, but rarely see Parker-Frost knives for sale.

Where do you see Frost Cutlery in the future?

I think that Frost Cutlery has a solid foundation; we have history, and we have a great name. I envision our growth continuing over the next few years. It is still a lot of fun for me and I know my son and daughter and Jeff really enjoy the business, so as long as they stay motivated along with me, I think that we will continue to grow as a pay-as-you-go operation. We have some unbelievable new ideas and new products coming out in the future.

What sets Frost Cutlery apart from the rest of the knife industry?

I feel that companies like Case and Buck build great knives, but their pricing structure is much higher than ours. We feel we build a great knife at a very reasonable price. Our Hen & Rooster brand has been going strong since 1845 and it has the history and the longevity to compete with Case and Buck.

For great value in a product, it's hard to beat knives from the Frost Cutlery and Steel Warrior lines. I think that is where we lead the industry. We have warranties against manufacturer's defects that we have honored for years.

We have always been the leader in commemorative knives. The backbone of all our commemoratives has always been the Dale Earnhardt editions, and from there we have fed off into other things. It has been a very good business for us for a number of years.

Tell us about Senior Vice President Jeff Daniel, who has been with you almost from the beginning.

When the business was still in its infancy in my garage, Jeff used to help me. When I went into the 400-square-foot building, he would come in after school to help. Jeff is really like family to me. He and his whole family are like that. They have been with me so long and he is a wonderful person.

I have often said that Jeff sets an example for other people. He is such a good person in the community, in his church and to his family. He is an example for people to follow and do well in life. I'm proud to have him in this company because everyone recognizes the type of person he is. He is amazing.

Why do you think your family and staff is so loyal?

People have ups and downs. Whenever people have their down periods, I have always tried to be there to help. Whether it's emotionally or financially, I try to be there for them. For as long as I can remember I have always wanted to help my fellow man. That desire had to have been instilled in me by my mother and father, and it is a blessing that they gave me a heart that makes me want to help other people.

Do you think it was the right choice to bring Stephen and Stefanie into the business?

Why are we here in life? We are here to contribute to mankind. I feel I have been fortunate to accomplish that mission through the lives of my son and daughter.

Stephen and Stefanie are like any young people in that they have their ups and downs over the years. But can you imagine being able to build a business like this and have both your son and daughter working in it with you? It is a wonderful thing. I get to see them almost every day and I have wonderful grandchildren.

Stephen and Stefanie are both very intelligent and hard working, and they are both great parents. I feel very fortunate because I never dreamed when I started in the lunch bucket that someday they would be in the business with me. I'm happy it all worked out that way.

What is your favorite pastime?

You know, my life has been consumed with work. That's been my life. When I was building Frost Cutlery, and even today, I would think nothing about coming in to work seven days a week. Once I start something, I live it, I love it and that's what I've done all my life.

I was working when my son was born. I was working fifty to eighty hours a week at the chemical plant, and sometimes more, because I got a lot of overtime pay. And then I would work on the side with the knives. So most of my life has been consumed by my real passion, which is my work.

I do like to fish, but that really came later in life. I didn't do

More to life than knives and softball: Tyler Pipes, son of Smoky Mountain Knife Works owner Kevin Pipes, and Jim Frost taking time out to fish for trophy rainbow trout.

Alexis Frost with her Poppy, Jim Frost, showing off the fresh catch of the day.

Sarah Peyton Durham, left, proudly shows off her catch. Sarah is Stefanie Frost-Durham's daughter.

Right, Poppy Jim Frost spending quality time on the lake with his grandkids, Pierce and Emerald Frost, who are son Steve's kids.

Terry Duncan, left, and his good friend, on-air talent and CCN host Todd Boone, proudly display a magnificent brown trout.

Jeff Daniel and man's best friend showing a nice rainbow trout landed while fly-fishing.

anything or go anywhere until my business was established. I never left the building, never left my work, until I had full confidence that everything would be fine if I walked out the door. Until then if someone wanted to meet with me, they had to come to me; I wouldn't take time away from work to go see them.

A different kind of fisherman: Jim and Jan's grandson, Conner Jones, with flippered friend.

I've got a lot of friends, but most of my free time has been spent with my family and especially with my son and my daughter as they came up playing sports. I spent an enormous amount of time on ball fields. I worked in youth leagues. I was president of youth leagues. I coached probably 1500 or better youth league ball games in basketball, football, baseball and softball. You have to make decisions in life as to what you're going to be involved in. I could have played golf, or I could have been a NASCAR fanatic, or I could have gone fishing on tour all the time. I could have done a lot of things, but the thing that I really enjoyed was working with my kids in sports—that was something that I really enjoyed.

You are famous throughout the world of girl's fastpitch softball as a pioneer of the sport and one of its most ardent supporters. Were you always interested in softball? Did you get involved with the sport because of your kids?

Yes, well at first I was involved in baseball with Stephen, when he was younger. But then Stefanie came along and when she was about five years old she started playing softball. As the years went by, through my involvement with her, I got more and more involved with the sport and, eventually, our Frost Falcons softball organization saw well over 200 student athletes get scholarships to good colleges. It has been very rewarding for me to have been able to participate in something that has created so much benefit for so many young people.

Chattanooga is considered the capital of girl's fastpitch softball in the Eastern United States. This is largely in part due to the city's magnificent Jim Frost Stadium, which has hosted the Southern Conference Softball Championship nine times since it opened in 1998. How did it feel to have this facility named in your honor?

I was humbled beyond belief. I usually like to do things quietly in the background, but in order to get this facility built I had to be out in front. It is a beautiful structure and I had no idea that they were going to name it in my honor. But the city, the county, UTC[2] and hundreds of other people all helped to make this dream possible, and so to have the stadium named after me was a very humbling experience.[3]

During the construction of the stadium, I met a lot of people I didn't know. I helped solicit funds and I discovered that this community is overrun with people with great hearts. This was an amazing time, not only in my company's history but also in mine.

You were the 2008 National Parks & Recreation Award Recipient.

Yes. It felt good to be honored, but in accepting the award I hoped to influence other people to get out and help advance the opportunities for student-athletes to get scholarships. I always say "student-athletes" because they are students first. There are an enormous number of scholarships available. I am for doing all that I can to help student-athletes reach their goals.

Has your involvement in softball and your role in building the Jim Frost Stadium provided opportunities for you to positively influence the lives of young people?

Yes, I have been blessed to be able to help a lot of young people,

---

2   University of Tennessee-Chattanooga.
3   Dedicated in 1998, this world class fastpitch softball stadium, conveniently located near the University of Tennessee-Chattanooga, was named in honor of Mr. Frost for his leadership and support in the construction of the facility.

and I am very fortunate in that area. But you know I've always felt that in this lifetime we are all on a journey, and I feel that I was destined to be involved in softball and to be able to have a hand in getting the Stadium built. In a way I think that being a part of getting the Stadium built did as much good for me and for Frost Cutlery as it did for the community and the thousands of young people who have played there.

You see, it took two years to get the stadium built and most of that time I was away from the business. But with Jeff Daniel and my son Stephen running the business, we actually prospered during that time and I began to realize that, whether I was here in the office or out working on the stadium, the business would continue without me.

Although it took a lot of time, money and effort on our part, I think building the stadium actually made our company much stronger, because it made Jeff and Stephen stronger. While I was busy with the stadium, they each had to step up and take on my responsibilities. They both shouldered the extra load with no complaints and took care of those additional responsibilities just like they had been doing it all of their lives. Since then I've had a lot of confidence in the direction Frost Cutlery will take after I'm gone. I have no doubt that the company will continue.

So everything has a purpose, no matter what it may be, and my philosophy is no matter what you do, it will come back to you.

Given your decades of involvement with the sport, we could no doubt fill a volume with your experiences in softball. Is there one particular anecdote you would like to share?

I coached over fifteen hundred softball games, but when Stephen was playing baseball I also coached boy's baseball teams. When Stephen was fourteen, we went down to Fort Oglethorpe, Georgia, to play a local team. Of course, they had furnished the umpire. We struggled throughout the ball game with the calls from behind the plate. The umpire was very tight with his calls when we were pitching and very loose when the other team was pitching.

Finally it came down to the last inning and we were up by a couple of runs. All of a sudden it didn't matter what we threw, the umpire would call it a ball. Our catcher would set up and call for a pitch right down the middle of the strike zone, waist high, the pitcher would hit the mitt dead center and the umpire would call it a ball. When we saw what was going on we started screaming and hollering about it, but it didn't make any difference; that umpire just kept walking batters until the bases were loaded.

I finally switched pitchers and put my son Stephen in to pitch. But still the umpire called every pitch he threw a ball and two runs came in on walks. Still the bases were loaded and the game was tied, so I called a time out. I went out on the field, called the team in to huddle, and I told them, "We're going to walk this next batter."

We went back out in the field. Stephen took the mound, the catcher stepped out to the right of home plate, and we threw ball one. The umpire looked at Stephen like, well what's going on here, but the next pitch was the same play, ball two. Now the umpire was looking at me like, you're crazy, what's going on, but the catcher stepped out again and Stephen threw him ball three. By that time everybody in the stands realized what was going to happen next and so they all started laughing at the umpire because he was being ridiculous.

The umpire called me over and said, "What's going on; what are you doing? This is the winning run."

"Mr. Ump," I said, "our team is going to determine who wins this ball game, not you." So we threw ball four and left the park.

Did showing that kind of personal integrity make a big impression on people, most especially your players?

Yes, and I think it made a big impression on that umpire, too.

What motivates you to be so generous to your friends, employees and to the citizens of this community?

I want to make everyone's life better. It is like on the *Cutlery Corner Network* cable television show when we give away knives. It's incredible sometimes that we can do what we do, that we can give away product. I know in my heart, I imagine on the other end, people opening up their boxes and getting those free gifts. I sometimes feel I can see their faces and hear people saying "I don't know how they do that!" I think that just excites me.

People who come through my door, whether they bought one knife thirty years ago or not, are always welcome to come back. I am always glad to see them. Those people put me where I am now. I have been involved with a lot of things for the community and I have said many times that I feel like I have a destiny in life. I feel like I have been placed here for a reason and I think I am utilized to do things to help other people.

I have a wonderful family, a wonderful business and I am still working 40-50 hours a week. People ask me, "Why do you work? Why are you still working?" I always say to them, "I have one goal in life: I hope that I can live and work for many more years because I'm going to be able to help that many more people." I believe that. That's how I feel inside. I think, "How many more can I help? If I live ten more years, how many more people, how many lives can I make better?"

What was your motivation for forming a charitable foundation?

The reason it was formed was to benefit student-athletes, whether it is for the construction of facilities that would benefit student-athletes or children in general. It has to be "child related." We use some of the funding for the T. C. Thompson Children's Hospital here in Chattanooga. I am especially proud of that.

If I have one goal in life it is to make our Charitable Foundation even stronger and more effective than it is now. My lifetime goal is to put large sums of money back into this community.

What is your greatest achievement?

About five years ago, when she was fifteen, my son's daughter, Alexis, was in intensive care at Children's Hospital. She went into cardiac arrest and the doctors in the Pediatric Care Unit told us they didn't know if she was going to live or die. But they worked hard to save her life and she's twenty years old now.

I was sitting in the waiting room and seeing the faces of the doctors and nurses as my granddaughter began to recover. They were so excited. It was almost like their feet weren't even touching the floor, all because they had saved this child.

I knew right then and there that I was going to do something. I didn't know what it was at the time, but I knew I was going to do something. At their next fund-raiser, I went down with Alexis and donated $100,000 to Children's Hospital.

You might ask, "What's so special about that?"

The special thing is that the hospital had a huge need in the Pediatric Care Unit and with that money; they can literally help thousands of children.

Alexis became a spokesperson for the Miracle Child Network here in Chattanooga. I believe the doctors and those nurses saved her life, and gave her back to us, because she was so close to death and they pulled her back from deaths door. Recently I had a meeting about enlarging the Pediatric Care Unit. Currently they are being forced to transport a lot of children to Atlanta, Nashville and Knoxville because they don't have enough room in the Pediatric Care Unit here in Chattanooga. They only have so many beds, and they need to expand their hospital for more. They needed additional monies to do that, so I committed another $50,000.

To me, my greatest achievement is the ability to be able to give in order to help all those kids. I will never know them, or know who my donations helped. It is the feeling you get down deep inside when you know you have contributed to mankind, when you know you have contributed to your community, that lets you know you've accomplished something truly worthwhile.

It is not for self satisfaction, it is to help others. Clearly, the opportunities I've been given to accomplish that stand out in my mind as my greatest achievements not because I did it, but because I was given the ability and the desire to do it.

MARGARET FROST
Mother of Jim Frost

Mrs. Frost, are there any stories about your son you would like to share?

One thing I always tell people is that Jim was very thrifty. He was a saver and he planned the things that he did with his money. When he first began his business he planned it out every step of the way.

Back in the old days, everybody cleaned house when spring came. You took the mattresses off the bed and the box springs, you cleaned everything, you got the dust off from everywhere in the house. You would sun the mattresses outside. One spring while Jim was still in high school, I took his mattress off his bed and there was all this money lying between the mattress and the box spring. It was money I had given him for lunch. Girls were always crazy about Jim and they fixed his lunch and brought it to him at school, so Jim saved that lunch money. He has made every dollar that he has ever made count for him.

Jim is really good. He loves softball, he loves being involved in it, and he loves the youth. He has helped so many young people—there's just nobody in this town who will ever know how many he has helped—who wanted to play ball, but didn't have the money to be involved. Jim has helped so many of them. He doesn't ask for recognition—he will accept it and he has been given a lot in this town, and out of town—but he is very humble, he is a very humble man. He enjoys what he does, it makes him feel good, it makes him feel worthwhile and it makes me extremely proud that he is my son.

Everybody in this town thinks the world of him. He gets recognized all the time and the City of Chattanooga just gave him an Honorary Certificate for his work.

Is Jim's story the Great American story?

It really is, because a lot of men have goals they want to reach but they don't all come true for them.

I have told Jim, "Every page you turn seems to turn to gold." It was never in my mind that his business would ever go as far as it has, and last as long as it has, but, knowing Jim, I'm not surprised because he gives his all to anything that he sets his head to go into. Jim doesn't venture into anything that he doesn't feel is going to work. He really has that knowledge about putting something together and he feels like it is going to work before he does it. He is a self-made man.

Jim's dad was just a country person, raised in Alabama, and he passed away in 1976. When Jim started the business, his dad said in his old low Alabama drawl, "Well I just don't understand all this knife business, one old pocketknife was all I ever needed." I think about that a lot. Jim's dad could never have visualized all the knives that his son has produced and sold and the many different types and kinds of knives and materials that he has used in the knives. His dad would have never in a million years thought that the business would come to where it is today.

As for me, well, I just knew that Jim was working hard, and I kept the children so he and his wife could travel at the time when he was first building his business. They knew the children were safe. [Laughing] I never did any spanking, I just sort of talked to them, and I would tell them, "Now you have to sit in the chair." That's what we used to always do. Now it's called "timeout." They were good children and they were not hard to keep at all.

If his father were alive today, would he be proud of Jim?

Oh, he certainly would. He might not understand it exactly and then again he might; I don't know. I do know that in his own way he was proud of Jim, but he was a man of few words.

You did a good job raising him.

I did my best to make a good boy out of Jim. So far he has lived up to the goals I had for him. I think Jim got most of it from me; his dad was a quiet person, he loved to fish and that was about it. I'm not trying to brag or anything, but I think he got most of his good business traits from me. The outgoing personality, the liking of people, and doing for others; that came from me. I love that boy and I would cook for him every day. I am sure he would sit his feet under my table every day, but he does have another life. He is just such a good boy, a good person, a good community leader. He loves the young people, and he loves doing for them. Jim would rather do for others than for himself, he is just that kind of a man. He has grown into a man and he has really made me proud of him in a lot of ways.

What can you tell us about Jim's ex-wife, Jo, who is also the mother of Stephen and Stefanie?

Jo has been very supportive of Jim and she has helped him in all his efforts. She is a very good organizer, she is a good person that knows how to put things together, and I know that Jim knows that and he gives her credit for it.

Jo and I get along very well. We have these children and grandchildren that are mine and hers. She is a grandmother and I am a great grandmother, and I have been with them, every one of them, since they were born. There is just really nothing, not anything bad that I would say about Jo, and I just think she has grown more and more helpful to Jim through the years. She will support Jim in whatever he does and do anything she can to help him.

Was the success of Frost Cutlery in the early years a direct result of her hard work?

Yes, she was a good supporter of Jim. Jo worked hard and was very helpful. Jim recognizes that, and he thanks her for it.

Are there any other Jim Frost antics the world needs to know?

Jim did play on the All-Star Team in football at Red Bank High School and he was the fastest runner on the team. He has loved sports all his life and he especially loved the football. His favorite team is the UT Vols. He hardly ever misses a game when they play at home in Knoxville. There is nothing hardly that goes on, sports-wise, that Jim is not involved in, especially if they need help.

In my mind, the way I see Jim, he would rather make money to spend it to help somebody else, than to do for himself. He could have any luxury item; you know, cars, condo in Florida. He could spend it all on himself, but he prefers to give to other people and that is what makes him happy. A lot of people in his position that make money, they give a little but they don't do anything like Jim Frost. You see all the upper echelon people, heads of those large companies that fill their pockets instead of helping the people in the country. To me, Jim Frost is a wise man. Even though he is my son, he is a wise man, and he has shown that by all the things that he has done.

Are you proud of him?

Just a little bit . . . I can't help it! He is a real good son in every way. I am so happy that things have worked out so well for him. I am a jokester. We joke with one another. He tries to call me on the phone, thinking he can disguise his voice and pull something on me. I just go along with it, but all the time I know it is him, I am his mother. Then I call him back and I will get him and I will say, "I got you that time, didn't I?" We have a lot of fun. He can't out-smart me.

What can you tell us about Jeff Daniel?

Jeff has been a really dedicated worker for Jim. They were neighbors for twenty years. Jeff went to work for Jim when he was in high school. His mother and dad are fine people. They are two people that would come to you even if they were on their sickbed to help you. We feel like Jeff is a son. He has been around so long, and been with Jim so long and he is such a good Christian boy. He loves his family, he loves to participate in his church and he is always ready to do anything helpful. He is a really helpful person and ready to do anything he can do for Jim and the company. He is a trustworthy person. I say that Jim has been able to take his company as far as he has because of the trustworthy people behind him like Jeff.

STEPHEN FROST
Son and Chief Operating Officer

What can you tell us about your dad?

He's a workaholic. He is very, very driven and goal oriented. Dad believes in luck, and in never delaying on anything. Certainly he is successful and well respected in the knife industry. I believe that much of his success can be attributed to his belief in always moving ahead without delay. When he has an idea, everyone in the company knows and respects his sense of urgency to get it done.

Stephen Frost

Work and business success is very important to Dad, and that is an ethic he instills in our family. For him, work is the fabric that supports and holds a family together, and what allows a family to be strong and prosper. Family and his work are extremely important to him, as well as being able to help others.

Dad is very good to the people around him. For as long as I can remember, my dad has wanted to do things for others, without expecting anything in return. Years ago, when he coached basketball and softball, if there was a kid who wanted to play, he would make sure that happened. If it meant putting in hours after his shift work to practice with them, or taking the time to pick someone up for practice, he was there. My dad has always been good to the kids he's known.

Are there any acts of generosity that stands out in your mind?

For me, Dad's generosity doesn't come down to a single deed or example; it is all of the little things he does everyday. Many people know about the softball stadium that Dad built for the UTC women's team. It has greatly impacted the lives of a lot of players by getting them exposure, and consequently, college scholarship opportunities. However, there are only a few people who know about the little things that I know. For example, years ago when I played basketball, my dad bought a guy on my team some basketball shoes that he needed. Another time, he paid for a girl who couldn't afford to go to softball camp. So, it isn't one thing that shows his generosity, but all of the little things he does that touches people's hearts and lives.

Why did you follow in your dad's footsteps?

It is really all I have ever known. When I was around fifteen, Jeff Daniel lived across the street from me, and we worked with my dad in the garage when the business was there. We helped him build a little shed, about ten by fifteen feet, behind the garage to store some of the products. Then I used to travel to all of the shows. Dad and I have always had a good working relationship. From the time he started the business, as the business was growing, and where the company is today; he and I have always been lucky to have such a good relationship. I believe it can be attributed to listening to one another. In the end, though, he has the last say-so, and that works well for us.

Seeing his success and all that he has been able to provide for my sister Stefanie and I, makes me want to follow in his footsteps. I hope that I will have the opportunity to do all of the things for my children that Dad has done for us.

What can you tell us about the early days of your dad's business?

At first, when Dad decided to make a business out of his hobby, the garage was continuously packed with products. Eventually, there were so many knives that we couldn't even store our bikes in there anymore. The knives were just overtaking everything. That is when we built the shed for more storage. It didn't take long before the shed was full, too, and we moved to the location on Airport Road.

Dad was always reinvesting the majority of the profits. The inventory was growing and the business was growing. It continued to outgrow one location after another, particularly during the Parker-Frost partnership. We were literally bursting at the seams of our facilities. It is amazing to see how far Frost Cutlery has progressed over the years. We have gone from buying, selling and trading knives from the back of a van, to selling thousands of knives around the world every day.

What part of dad's business do you consider to be the most interesting?

It's neat to see all these people like Eddie Jessup, Ken Griffey, Kevin Pipes, and Phil Martin, who were just ordinary guys buying knives out of my dad's van, who are now leaders in a multimillion dollar industry. We were a major part of that growth. If you were to go back in time and tell me all of us would be where we are today, I would tell you that you were crazy.

What do you think sets Frost Cutlery apart from other companies?

There are several things that I believe have made Frost Cutlery an exceptional company in the industry. First of all, it has always been our goal to ship every order on the day that it is received. At times this has been a tall order, and we have still been shipping orders at nine or ten o'clock at night. It is our philosophy that shipping the orders out in a timely way, keep our customers ordering and re-ordering.

Secondly, we make customer service our top priority. Customers get their merchandise quickly, they get a quality product, and if there are any issues they are addressed and resolved immediately. We always make sure that the customers are satisfied with their experience with our company.

Thirdly, we offer exceptional products at the most competitive prices. My dad has always bargained very keenly with vendors to ensure that we are getting the best merchandise for our customers at the best possible price. Our customers reap the benefits of this bargaining. In addition, we are constantly bringing new product lines and commemorative items into the marketplace. This all sets Frost Cutlery apart, and make us one of the leading companies in the industry.

Was there a moment in your life when you realized that your dad was a great man and what he was doing was special?

I can't say there was one moment in particular but a series of moments. I would say multiple times throughout my life I realized that something special was happening, and Dad was an essential part of it. When you are younger you don't realize or appreciate what's going on around you. It's not until you get older do you truly start to see things as they really are and the impact it has on people's lives around you.

As more and more national tournaments come to Chattanooga and the city grows in prominence in women's softball, you can directly attribute that to Dad's influence. Obviously building the stadium was a center piece of that success. Knowing that my dad was a major catalyst in making that come to fruition makes it special.

But to answer your question, I can say over the last two years as I have now taken on the responsibilities of coaching, business, family and community, much like Dad did back in those early days, I have come to truly appreciate all the hard work it took for him to juggle all of it. I realize what effort it took to keep it all together, balancing time versus commitments and the team versus the business. It was quite an exceptional achievement. I hope it's something I can achieve as well.

What has your dad done to help you better your life?

The greatest thing he has done to help me is just he being himself. His dedication, his desire, doing what he says he is going to do and the drive he has to complete his goals has been a major influence of me and my life. Being able to perceive what's happening around you, recognizing what needs to be done and what can be done are traits that he has passed on to me.

Keeping with the philosophy of "working off our own money" and "paying as we go" are two principles that I will never deviate from. It worked for him, it works for me and it will continue to work for this company after Dad is gone.

STEFANIE FROST-DURHAM
Daughter and Executive Director

What can you tell us about your father?

He feels he is very blessed and his mission in life is to give back. He sets goals for himself to help our community and works very hard to reach those goals. He has a gift fund he uses to make contributions to organizations such as T. C. Thompson Children's Hospital, University of Tennessee Knoxville, University of Tennessee Chattanooga, and many more organizations.

Stefanie Frost-Durham

Do you have a favorite Frost Cutlery story?

Years ago, when I was in middle school, he arranged for the local children's home to provide him with a wish list for each of the children's Christmas. He bought each child exactly what they wanted and had a luncheon at work in their honor.

Is this typical of your dad?

Yes, he has a heart of gold. One of my favorite Dad stories is when my dad found a family whose home had burned and was in a lot of need. He got a meal together for them and gifts for the kids. It was Christmas-time and we took Christmas to them. Those are the kind of things he does all year long.

He has given an extremely generous donation to [T. C. Thompson] Children's Hospital. They were so happy to bring us down and see what the money had helped them accomplish. While we were there he noticed the waiting room needed an updated TV and in the next couple weeks he had a 42" flat screen TV delivered and installed. Being able to help others is a driving force in his work ethic.

"You probably think that I cut down this tree with this Frost Cutlery 'Bowie' knife."

"I didn't. But if I *had to try* with a 'Bowie' knife, this would be the one I would use."

Frost Cutlery Survival Bowie (10-189) 13-1/2" overall length; features a hollow handle with a liquid filled compass and 440 Stainless Steel blade. Comes with an all leather sheath. Retail: $66.00

Available at Cutlery World Stores nationwide.

Stephanie Frost advertising for her dad and his company.

Are you and your brother following in your dad's footsteps?

We definitely have big shoes to fill, but I hope we are. He has instilled in us the value of giving, caring, seeing the needs of others, sharing your good fortune with others, realizing the gifts God has given you, and always looking for the best in others.

I played softball and my dad was the coach and sponsor of our team. He also sponsored several other teams, and still does. He always made sure every player had cleats, a bat, helmet, and gloves. He helped us with fundraisers for tournament costs. We could go from door to door selling Frost Cutlery knives, all the teams he sponsored would. Each team would get 100% of the knife sales. The community actually looked forward to our fundraisers so they could buy a new Frost Cutlery knife. If our fundraisers left some of the team members short for traveling expenses for tournaments he would cover their additional expenses.[4]

Did your dad ever miss your practices or games?

That is one thing my mom praised my dad about. He never missed anything. He would make sure that, no matter what, he attended everything my brother and I participated in. We were very lucky that it was so important to him to be there for us. I feel very lucky and blessed I am able to work with him, that I am able to see him as often as I do. He is the same way with his grandkids. He doesn't miss a thing they participate in. Family is very important to him.

Does he do things for himself, for recognition?

No he doesn't. There are so many people out there that are motivated by recognition, but Dad is not. It is the joy he gets from helping others that drives him. He believes every person has a value, and he sees that, and helping is his way of giving back. He is known for saying "those who seek, listen, learn, and utilize the intelligence of others, are themselves the smartest people."

---

4   On average, 10-12 teams per year are sponsored

What do you think about the protective nature of the employees of your dad's reputation?

You have to admire a man who inspires such loyalty. Not just anyone can motivate people like he does. His charisma and influence tends to have such sway with the people, not just employees but in the community as well. He is so goal oriented and driven, that I would not want to be the one standing in his way of him achieving his goals. I can only imagine the obstacles he faced when he was trying to get the stadium built, and how he had to negotiate with people who represented those challenges. Even though he faced roadblocks; detours; and some resistance, the final destination has been great for the community. The employees know in order for Dad to be an effective community leader his reputation and that of the company's is of the most vital importance.

Was there a moment in your life when you realized that your dad was a great man and what he was doing was special?

I can't say there was just one moment but several moments when I knew he was doing something great. You can look at the softball trophy case [inside Frost Cutlery headquarters] and just imagine all the girls that went through the Frost Falcons softball program and had opportunities to go to college. He will never know all the lives he has touched, but it's never been about the recognition and that's what makes him unique.

There is always something happening where he is trying to help someone or some organization. People regularly come to him for help and he is always ready and willing to give. I can't think of anyone he ever turned down.

What has your dad done to help you better your life?

Instilling in me his driven nature is his greatest gift in my life. If he wasn't so driven, I wouldn't be so driven. My son, Charlie, probably wouldn't be here if I wasn't persistent in following up with the doctors and making the phone calls to the different specialists about his condition. You have to give God the glory and I thank Him also for my father who taught me to never give up, never let someone tell you that you can't do something.

He has also been a great source of encouragement for my husband and me, especially with starting our own business, Durham Design. He has given me all these tools to use but also the opportunity to put them into everyday practice. His goal for me and my life was no matter what I chose to do that I would be prepared to be independent and self-sustaining.

Stefanie's children, Charlie and Peyton.

Do you think that you will follow in your father's footsteps?

I can't say for sure at this moment. Gunner[5] and I are in the early stages of building our family, starting our business and structuring our lives and that of our children. Stephen's life very much parallels that of Dad's but he is very much his own person with his own set of priorities and life path. Is it my goal to be a professional business woman and mother juggling career, family, coaching and community? Not at the moment but you never know what the future holds, or what God has planned for your life. My father has lived a very prosperous and fruitful life. I would be honored and lucky for my life to be able to follow a similar path as his. I can't rule out the possibility but where we are now it's too soon to tell where life is taking us.

---

5   Stefanie's husband, Gunner Durham

JEFF DANIEL
Senior Vice President

How did you become Frost Cutlery Company employee number one?

My journey with Mr. Frost began long before the journeys of most of those who know him today. As a kid I lived across the street from his house, and as I grew up, my desire to make money doing odd jobs landed me several opportunities at Mr. Frost's home. Mowing the grass, cleaning out gutters, trimming bushes, painting fences and even

Jeff Daniel

babysitting Stefanie helped propel me on my own entrepreneurial path.

Before long Mr. Frost's business began to flourish and he presented me with an opportunity that changed my life.

He met me in the street one afternoon when the school bus had dropped me off after school, and asked if I would consider working for him in the evenings, shipping orders out of his garage and helping keep up with inventory.

"Now let me get this straight," I said. "You mean I get to work for you, shipping knives in the evenings after school, and I get paid for it?"

It was a no-brainer. I said "Yes" and even though I was just a teenager that decision was one of the biggest and best I ever made.

What can you tell us about the early days of Frost Cutlery?

My first actual job was picking and packing orders for shipments to Mr. Frost's customers. The inventory at that time fit on a three-inch ledge that surrounded the interior of his garage. The ledge was formed by concrete blocks protruding from the foundation of the house. The orders were pulled and moved to a makeshift packing station in the garage, where they were invoiced and logged into the United Parcel Service book for pick up each day. Some days were busier than others,

60

some orders were bigger than others, but every order received the same priority treatment: They all went out the same day they were received. (Today, we still strive to ship orders the same day they are received, but there are times when that is logistically impossible.) After a few years of making do with inventories stacking off the ledge and onto the floor of the garage, a much needed office space was added to the back of the house. This sufficed for a short time but it was really just a Band-Aid where we needed a tourniquet.

The business began to grow at a steady pace and soon more space was needed just to hold inventories of shipping supplies. To meet the need a small storage shed was located on Lee Highway—five miles from our homes—and rented. The business continued to grow and soon Mr. Frost had to make decisions about how to move forward and about the security issues that resulted from having a knife business located in his home. Finally, those realities forced the first big move for Frost Cutlery, out of the Frost home to a place of rented commercial suites. One suite served as Mr. Frost's office and the other became my warehouse. We still kept our shipping materials stored offsite in our storage shed, which was now seven miles from our new location.

As business grew, so did the demand for additional warehouse space. The building we were in had a total of four suites located side by side. We occupied two of the four suites, both of which were located side-by-side on one end. As fate would have it, when additional space became a necessity, the only one of the four units available was the suite at the end opposite from ours, with another business located in

Frost Cutlery's first office and warehouse suites.

the suite between us. We took it anyway and the business continued to grow. Soon, and as if having to go outside and down the sidewalk just to fill orders didn't complicate matters enough, we ended up having to rent space across town, in Hixson, Tennessee, which required at least a 30-minute round trip drive, depending on what time of the day you had to make that trip. Maybe we had lost our minds or maybe we were just in survival mode. Either way, not having a loading dock, a forklift or a pallet jack meant that the large wooden crates full of knives delivered by trucks to our front door had to be unloaded by hand and broke down in the parking lot, just to get them to fit through the door of our "warehouse" suite.

What were some of the challenges in those early days?

My father—my hero and my inspiration—always had a saying that it is better to work smarter, not harder. That day finally arrived when we built our first building and consolidated our three suites, our shipping supplies storage shed building, and our rented warehouse space across town. Man, was I ever in hog heaven! At last I had a large, new warehouse with my own loading dock and, one of my best purchases to date, a new pallet jack.

There is a lot of wisdom in working smarter, not harder, and it paid off for Frost Cutlery. In what seemed like only a few years, a new expansion had to be added to our existing building in order to provide still more warehouse storage. Soon, thereafter we were overflowing with product again. One evening, in the new section of the

The first commercial building owned by Frost Cutlery.

warehouse, we had so much inventory that our shelving buckled under the strain, twisted and then collapsed like dominoes. A horrific noise and a tangled mess announced a new challenge. Fortunately, no one was working

Jan Watson, Jim Frost and Jeff Daniel in a staff meeting.

in the back warehouse, when our neatly stacked and organized warehouse, came tumbling down. Much to our dismay, our already packed warehouse had to be moved temporarily into the aisles of the undamaged section of the warehouse, making routine pulling and shipping procedures nearly impossible, while new, more robust shelving systems were being installed.

Again, I heard Mr. Frost's soon-to-become-ubiquitous mantra, "I don't want to get any bigger." However, that is not such an easy mandate when you have a subtle yet very aggressive owner pushing you to be the best you can be. Throw in the fact that Frost Cutlery sells excellent quality products at a very reasonable price and backs them up with a limited lifetime guarantee, and you have a great recipe for success in business.

Frost Cutlery headquarters and addition was the company's second commercial building.

Do you think Jim Frost is truly a gifted salesman or just plain lucky?

Both! Maybe luck has something to do with Frost Cutlery's success, too, and Mr. Frost will readily admit that he has lucky green underwear. That's too much information for sure but maybe there is something to it. Seeing that "everything he touches turns to gold" seems to come true so often, Mr. Frost's good fortune and his beloved green underwear gave birth to one of his other nicknames, Lucky, which has since evolved to Uncle Lucky. Call it whatever you like, the facts are that Frost Cutlery has been propelled to a leadership position in the knife industry by a shrewd and frugal businessman whose agenda is established according to his own views about how to conduct business.

One of the keys to Mr. Frost's success is his incredible talent for numbers. You better have your numbers correct when dealing with Mr. Frost, because he can recall from memory what he paid for a specific knife and what the exchange rate was at the time of its purchase. He's from the old school, which taught him to crunch numbers in his head faster than I can with a calculator or computer. I have seen him walk away from a deal for several thousand knives because he had done the math in his head and figured out that our supplier was a nickel higher than he felt he could pay.

It may have been a lot of those nickels saved that allowed us to step out in faith and break ground on our next new building in May of 1989. The metal and block building was designed to be 25,200 square feet, with 6,000 square feet of that allocated to office space. As the new building neared completion, I drove my car into the middle of the warehouse. I sat there in my car and tried to imagine not only the layout, but what we would ever do with so much space. It was a far cry from the 2-inch ledge that ran around the perimeter of the Frost's garage on Mary Dupre Drive and once supported our complete inventory.

After moving in to the new facility, what did you do with the extra space until it was utilized?

We had so much space in our new building that we dedicated a portion of the warehouse to batting cages, as well as pitching rubbers and fielding stations where kids could train year round rain or shine. Later, when warehouse space once again became a premium, Mr. Frost not only continued to offer his training facilities to his Frost Falcons teams, he also allowed other teams—even competitors—to use the facilities free of charge.

Instead of moving the practice cages out of our warehouse so we could have enough room to operate the business, Mr. Frost decided the only logical thing to do was to add on to the existing building. So in 1997 a new addition was designed and built, with a lot of help from innovative architects, softball coaches, players' parents and, of course, Mr. Frost's wisdom and visionary thinking. We were able to open the new facilities just in time for the USA Women's World and Olympic fastpitch softball champions to practice and train prior to an exhibition game in Chattanooga. Some of the world's most famous softball players practiced in our warehouse, including Lisa Fernandez, Dr. Dot Richardson, Laura Berg, Gillian Boxx, Sheila Cornell, Michele Granger, Lori Harrigan, Dionna Harris, Kim Maher, Leah O'Brien, Julie Smith, Michele Smith, Shelly Stokes, Dani Tyler, Christa Williams, Jennifer Brundage, Barbara Jordan, Jennifer McFalls, Martha O'Kelley and Michelle Venturella. They were coached by legendary Olympic softball coach Ralph Raymond, a member of the National Softball Hall of Fame, along with assistant coach and Mr. Frost's longtime friend, Ralph Weekly.

What can you tell me about Jim Frost's contributions to women's sports and the community?

Mr. Frost was instrumental in bringing Karen and Ralph Weekly to Chattanooga to be the cohead coaches of the University of Tennessee-Chattanooga's women's fastpitch softball team, the Lady Mocs. His love for the game and his vision of building a world class softball stadium was shared by the Weekly's, who built a very competitive program at UTC. The two cohead coaches were not only able to see the vision that Mr. Frost shared with them, they also helped bring the vision to fruition. So the three visionaries worked together to create a

Right: Aerial view of Frost Cutlery's 100,000-square-foot warehouse located in Ooltewah, Tennessee. Since this photo, the facility has been expanded and now covers 150,000 square feet. Above: Inside the warehouse.

world class softball facility, Jim Frost Stadium, located in Chattanooga's Warner Park. There, on virtually any sunny day, you can drive by and see young student athletes playing a game Mr. Frost so dearly loves.

Jim Frost Stadium would not have become a reality without the support of the City of Chattanooga and its Parks & Recreation department, the Hamilton County government, Mr. Dennis Riddle, President of Komatsu America Corp., and, most important, the local community. Mr. Frost often says it is imperative to surround yourself by good people and that if you do, good things will happen. Chattanoogans are truly blessed to have a strong core group of good people who are committed to the care and well-being of the city and its surroundings, as well as to its youth and the future of our community, and the new stadium is a symbol of such commitment. On the 20th of April, 1998, the inaugural game was played in Jim Frost Stadium, between the Lady Mocs of the University of Tennessee-Chattanooga and the powerhouse Lady Vols of the University of Tennessee in Knoxville. The long-awaited day saw sellout crowds with standing room only, all hoping to catch a glimpse of history being made. The buzz in the air and the excitement from the players and fans alike was a confirmation, a confirmation not of boastful pride, but of gratitude for the benefits that so many would derive because of the Stadium, from the spectators who would enjoy being able to watch in comfort and safety, to the young student athletes who would play in a world class stadium, a Stadium of 1,000 Dreams that has hosted and continues to host softball games for all ages and abilities.

Teams travel from all over the United States to play in softball tournaments held in Chattanooga, with many of the games played in the Stadium. I often say that softball is our main business and the knife business is just a cover-up.

As impressive as Mr. Frost's support of the sport of softball may seem whether in helping a local high school, a small college or a large university, or in building sports training complexes or a world class softball stadium it is only the tip of the iceberg that is his generosity. For example, local hospitals have received not just monetary donations from Mr. Frost but other, thoughtful contributions, such as a new widescreen TV installed in a Children's Hospital waiting room to help ease the anxious tension of worried parents and other loved ones.

On another occasion, at Mr. Frost's direction I took part of our IT department to a local high school to set up classrooms with new computers. Like I said, these examples are just the tip of the iceberg, and like an iceberg it is what has been hidden from view, the many anonymous gifts or donations Mr. Frost has been able to give, that has resulted in some of Mr. Frost's favorite stories, and mine. Some of those stories would make you laugh and some would wrench at your heart, but all of them would tell of an extraordinary man who has been richly blessed by being able to help others by giving in so many ways.

Do you think that knife sales or the need for pocketknives will ever end?

One would think that by now we have sold everybody a couple dozen knives for their collection, a block set for the kitchen, a set of steak knives, a sword to hang on the wall, a couple hunting or skinning knives for their gear, commemorative knives to show off, and a few favorite pocket knives to carry or trade. Apparently that hasn't been the case, because during a warm, sunny week in July 2002, we moved in to a capacious 100,000-square-foot warehouse that we built on our campus in Ooltewah, Tennessee, just a stone's throw away from the Chattanooga city limits. Since then, another addition has been required to help sustain a seemingly unending influx of business. This brings our current facilities to a total of 150,000 square feet, housing millions of dollars worth of inventory and 150 sales and warehouse associates.

ROBERT SIMPSON
Former Salesman and Oldest Customer

Mr. Simpson, you are now more than eighty years old and you were one of the first salesmen for the Parker-Frost knife company. But we understand you are also one of the first customers of Frost Cutlery.

I went to work for Parker-Frost in March of 1977 as a salesman. Mr. Parker and Mr. Frost hadn't been together as partners for too long, but I had fooled around with knives for a long time before then. I had also worked in the leather industry since 1955.

I went up and talked to Jim Parker and Jim Frost, and after I talked with them for a while, I told them, "I don't know if I can make a living selling knives."

Mr. Parker said, "It might fool you," and so we agreed on what he'd pay me and all that stuff and where I would travel, and I went to work for them. I have never looked back. That's one thing Mr. Parker would always tell me: "Never look back."

When I first went to work for Parker-Frost, Mr. Parker said, "I would just as soon that you don't go over into West Tennessee." You know he had a big distributor over there, and a few years later he set his brother John Parker and some other guys up at Smoky Mountain Knife Works. We got them started in the knife business, and in time they became one of the biggest knife companies in that region.

What Parker-Frost really wanted me for was to sell new products. I didn't know about old knives, or what Mr. Parker called collector knives and I enjoyed that.

What happened after the Parker-Frost split?

I stayed with Parker until he bought the W. R. Case & Sons Cutlery Company and a nationwide retail outlet that finally put him under. The retail outlet was slated for bankruptcy when Mr. Parker bought it and he never recovered from that.

After that, I went into business for myself and I started buying whatever I could buy. Most of my stuff came from Mr. Frost. He had some items that I sold, and Frost and I were pretty good buddies.

Why did you buy your knives from Frost Cutlery?

I knew those boys pretty well, Mr. Parker and Mr. Frost. They were good people, and I liked both of them. I made a good living. I have never regretted going into the knife business.

Do you still buy knives from Frost Cutlery to resell?

There's a flea market down in Alabama that I go to every Saturday, for at least the last thirty years now. I'll buy some knives today and take them with me to Alabama. I have a few customers down there who will buy anything new from W.R. Case.[6]

When I first started selling knives at that flea market, if I had a dozen knives in a satchel, I was doing pretty well. But now I have to get help to unload my van. I don't know if anybody told you but when Parker and Frost first started out, they put their stuff in the back of a car and went to flea markets. There was a flea market in Nashville, and one of my customers that I sold knives to had a booth there. My customer didn't go up on Fridays; he waited until Saturday and Sunday. Parker and Frost went up on Friday and used his booth [to sell from on] Friday night, then [my] customer took over on Saturday.

Anything else you remember, Mr. Simpson?

Mr. Frost asked me one day, "You remember that day you were over at my garage buying some stuff, and when you left me I was crying?"

I told him, "I don't know anything about that."

He said, "You came over there and told me that I was selling to someone else cheaper than to you and you told me what to do with it! Then you walked off. I really was, I was crying, when you left there."

---

6   Frost Cutlery sells standard Case brand knives as well as customized Case knives featuring Corelon handles and special engraving.

KEVIN PIPES
Owner, Smoky Mountain Knife Works

How did you get into the knife business?

We got into the knife business because John Parker and I sold Indian Artifacts together. Jim Frost and Jim Parker sold knives. I bought a commercial building for John and me to start selling our Indian Relics. John asked Jim what he thought about the idea, and Jim said, "I think it's a good idea, but what you need to do is to sell the knives alongside with your Indian relics and you can pay us when you sell them."

How could we lose in that kind of a deal? So we agreed to start selling knives and Parker-Frost gave us $20,000 worth of knives on a consignment basis. When we opened up that small retail store, which was about 800 square feet, we had knives on one side and arrowheads on the other side. Everybody that came in bought the pocketknives and didn't even look at the arrowheads.

From left to right, Jim Frost, Chase Pipes, Kevin Pipes (owner, Smoky Mountain Knife Works), Tyler Pipes and Steve Frost, checking out Blade Master sharpening kits.

Would you say your learned the trade from Parker-Frost?

Probably the first thing to say, when people ask me what college I went to, I always laugh and tell them, "I went to Parker-Frost Tech." And "I'm a graduate of Parker-Frost Tech." I guess in saying that—what I mean is over the years and especially in the initial years of my business career selling pocketknives, I would always seem to learn a new lesson from Jim Frost and also from Jim Parker on a regular basis. When I thought I knew everything there was to know, usually Jim Frost or Jim Parker (because at that time they were partners) would teach me a new marketing strategy or lesson.

What can you tell us about Jim Frost?

I have known Jim for almost thirty years now. What has always impressed me about with Jim is that he does a lot for the community he believes in. He has done a lot for individuals, but he always did it without trying to make anyone feel that he was somebody better than anybody else. Once Jim told me that he puts his pants on every day just like everybody else. That is quite remarkable for someone who has been as successful as he.

Jim's background is similar to mine. He went into the knife business as a side job, applied his natural ability watched it become successful. He had a unique ability to envision what people wanted and he always recognized his customer. I think these are some of the things that made Frost Cutlery so successful. Another is that he offers a good value pocketknife for a great value for the money. He also acquired the Hen & Rooster trademark, a venerable old brand which he was able to develop to an even higher level.

Most important, Jim, like me, has involved his children in this business. The next generation is going to come along and have the values that he has taught them. Just like me these kids will say, "I went to Parker-Frost Tech." I learned a lot of the same lessons that Jim's kids have learned. I watched Jim and tried to learn from him every day.

Jim has a lot of strong personal values that are good for our country. I have never called him up and asked for a donation for a knife club and been turned down. Likewise, Smoky Mountain Knife Works is the same way. This is the kind of commitment to country and community that makes America strong. Jim is really a fantastic human being.

Scott Combs
Purchasing Agent

What do you do at Frost Cutlery?

I help Jim with all the purchasing of the knives for the company to resell. I go overseas to China and Germany to look for new innovative products and ideas, and help design new stuff right there on the spot.

How did you meet Jim Frost?

I actually met Jim roughly twenty-eight years ago, when his daughter Stefanie first started playing softball. She played for my mother's team. That is when he got into softball. Later, when I went to work for Frost Cutlery, my first job was packing swords—and I packed quite a few! It was right before we started selling to a large shopping network. We could sell a lot of swords every night on that television show because they had such a large audience.

About three years before I started working for Jim, I stopped at a drive-thru with the wife and kids and I saw him walking in and I said, "What are you doing over this way?"

He just hollered, "Hello!" back at me and went on in.

I got my food and started to pull out of the drive-thru and he hollered at me to stop. He walked over to my car and said, "Here, go get your kids some toys," and handed me two hundred dollars.

I said, "What did you do that for?" and he said, "Those kids need some toys." He hadn't seen me in ten years at that point.

I have watched that man walk over and hand a kid a $100 bill, just because that is the way he is. I mean, Jim will go into his pocket to help any child. It is unreal, watching what he will do. Another time there was a kid selling stuff to raise money and Jim just walked over and dumped a hundred dollar bill in the kid's box and walked off. Not long ago I was down at Erlanger Hospital in Chattanooga installing a 42-inch flat-screen television that Jim donated to the Children's wing for the parents' waiting room.

What is it like to work with Jim Frost on purchasing products?

If you throw numbers at him, stay away from numbers, because he will burn you. It is unreal, he does not forget numbers. He can tell you what he paid for something ten years ago, his memory is phenomenal. Jim likes to see a picture of the product with a number. He can remember the numbers but the picture makes it easier. That way if someone asks later, "Did we order this?" he can point to the picture and say, "Yeah, right here it is."[7]

In addition to our imports, we also buy knives from domestic sources. If we see something that is different, or unique, we will try it. Jim likes the weird and unique patterns. All I know is if it is going to sell, then we are going to run with it. Also, the knife makers/vendors actually come visit us at our offices. They bring catalogs and samples and a lot of times they will airfreight their samples to us.

Do you purchase much from China as well?

Yes, we go to a trade show in China sometimes. It doesn't matter if we go in April or October; it is twenty-one days because of the way the show runs. We are there for the whole show, and the way flights run out of China, you have to stay until the last two days of the show to catch a flight. It is the world's largest fair for goods of all kinds. Jim and I went over there about five years ago to place the first order for Steel Warrior, a product line of Frost Cutlery Knives. Jim said, "How are we going to explain to them what we want?"

I took a couple of Hen & Rooster pieces and said, "This is how we will do it."

I showed those pieces to the Chinese manufacturers and said to them, "I want it done with this quality."

They looked at the knives. The inside of the Hen & Rooster knife is polished and they took one look at it and said, "We can do that." The actual pattern I gave them is a #351 pattern in Hen & Rooster, which is the #123 pattern in Steel Warrior. Those are the patterns they first

---

7   Mr. Frost utilizes a file cabinet full of 3-ring binders containing pictures or color photographs and other order details of many of the knives he purchases for Frost Cutlery.

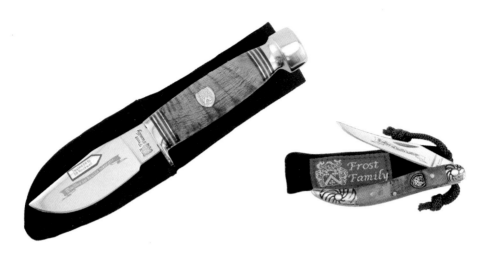

Frost Family brand pocket knife and fixed blade. Each of these knives proudly bears the Frost family crest and their blades are etched with the Latin motto, *Qualitas est familia institutio*, which means: "Quality is a family tradition."

started with.

Later, we were driving down the road in east-wherever China and Jim said to me, "I want to do a Frost Family Series."

I said, "Why don't you use your family crest for the knife shield?"

Jim laughed and said, "That is why I keep you around!"

Describe the coloring process for bone handles.

There are a couple of ways that it is done. One way is to wipe on stain and there is another process that involves boiling. Staining bone is just like staining wood. If you take a piece of wood and wipe stain on and wipe it right back off, it is going to be light in color. If you wipe it on and let it sit for five or six minutes, then wipe it off, it is going to be darker in color. This is the same way with bone.

Our main supplier of our bone in Pakistan provides dyed bone to manufacturers all over the world. First he boils the bone to extract all the oils and then he boils it in a color dye for up to two weeks. Then he takes the whole bone out and when it is sanded and polished, the color has soaked all the way through it. Other manufactures dye just the top, like a stain. Some of our vendors in China are learning this

Hen & Rooster Bowie knife pictured with a leather sheath. This collector's edition commemorates the 165th anniversary of one of the Frost family of brands.

boiling process and they have been working with it. Each color, to get the richness, depends on how long it is boiled. We have done a little bit of every color. We have done purples, variations of reds and it has all sold. We have even done pink bone-handled knives, and some of the reds come in a little pink because of the bone density.

What about the Corelon handle material?

Corelon is a hardened acrylic resin that is poured by hand. For example if you want red, white and blue, the makers take a cookie sheet, pour one color in and then pour the next color. They pour it by consistency of the color. Some colors, like black, will take over everything, so whichever color is more dominant they use less. They will take a special instrument and drag it back and forth in the poured material to make an "S" or some other shape.

JERRY LAWHORN
Retail Showroom Manager (Retired)

Tell us about Jim Frost.

If you met Mr. Frost on the street you would think that he is just as normal a five-days-a-week working man as you would ever see. You wouldn't know that he is so successful, such a big businessman and that he is just as good as gold. But Jim has done a lot, not only for Chattanooga but he has also helped a lot of girls get scholarships in softball. When he was coaching the teams he worked real hard on getting those girls college scholarships.

Jerry Lawhorn showing off a Hen & Rooster collection.

I have been with Jim for twenty-seven years, so you can say that I have been pretty happy to work for him, and he has treated me like a brother for all those years. When I first started with Jim there were only four employees. We have grown so much and the reason is because he has a smart head on his shoulders. Jim never does anything half way; he always does it right. He is a real smart man when it comes to business, probably one of the best in Chattanooga and probably all over Tennessee and a lot of other states.

Jim has earned everything that he has got. I'm talking about the notoriety, the wealth and the friendships with people all around the city and the state. People know him all over the United States, not only because of his knife business but also because he sponsors girl's fastpitch softball teams. He is a really good man and he would do anything for anybody. He is truly one-of-a-kind.

Everything Jim touches goes good; it doesn't go bad. Anything he does, whatever he gets into, he does it right. For example, a while back I talked to him about opening a showroom to the public and he said, "I don't know if it will work or not." But then he said, "I tell you what; leave some tables out and we will see how it goes."

The next thing you know, just by word of mouth, people were coming in every day. Every single day people visited our store. I had regular customers that came every single week. The customers come from California, Ohio, Florida and Arizona, and from all over the United States. A lot of times when they are going south they stop in here because they want to see the company and buy a few knives.[8]

What impresses me is that, because Frost Cutlery is a big business, people came in here wanting donations for their organizations. I have not yet one time seen Jim turn anybody down. He called me and said "Jerry give them two or three dozen knives for their organization." People came in here all the time for donations and he has never said no to them. Jim always gives them something to help their fund raiser. In my opinion, and many others, Jim Frost is the best around this city.

8   Something fairly new for Frost Cutlery is their open-to-the-public store attached to their shipping department/warehouse area.

BOB JOHNSTON
Phone Sales/Personnel/Warehouse Manager

Tell us about Jim Frost.

Jim was the best man at my wedding and I was the best man at his wedding. He and I were friends a long time before I came to work here.

Jim talks the talk and he walks the walk. One time I watched a guy mess over him in a business deal. The guy just did something he shouldn't have done. I said to Jim, "I bet you are upset."

He said, "I am really disappointed, I really am, but I tell you what; I'm not going to let it get me down today."

I said, "It will get me down for the rest of the week."

Jim said, "You know me better than that, if his kid needed an operation, I would give him the money for it."

There is the difference. Jim isn't just talking. One time, there was a situation that no one knows about. There was a business associate of Jim's that he and his wife were talking to, and it was obvious that this guy was ill, very ill. Jim asked what the problem was and the man told Jim, "Well, we don't have the money to go to the doctor."

Jim asked, "What do you mean?"

And the guy said, "I don't want to go to the doctor unless I can pay for it, but we have a deal coming soon and then we will be able to pay for it."

Jim reaches into his pocket handed him some money and said, "You are going to take this money, and you are going to go to the doctor or we are not going to do any more business, and there is only one thing; you can't ever tell me how much money this was."

Now I happen to know how much money Jim had on him; he had $5,000 in one pocket. Now, he normally doesn't carry a lot of money, but on this particular day he had some money. That is pure Jim Frost.

Let me tell you one of my favorite stories. My wife and Jim are good friends and they pick on each other a great deal. They have fun kidding each other all the time. About twelve years ago, we and our wives went skiing. Now Jim had been skiing before, but I had not; I was born and raised in Tennessee and slapping two pieces of lumber on my feet and sliding off an icy mountain is not my idea of having fun.

Anyway, the first day Jim and I went up the mountain thirteen times. It was a disaster, but he taught me how to ski. People were laughing at me. A lot of rich folks were there and there were also a few movie stars around. It was one of those high dollar places. Me being the hillbilly I am, I was more or less like a mascot around there; if only I had been wearing a plaid ski jacket or overalls!

Jim and I had come down to the bottom of the hill and we were standing in line to go back up. All of these people had been skiing since they were five years old, everybody was rich, except me, and there must have been a hundred people waiting to get on this chair-lift thing, and I fell and busted my butt. Now you don't do that, that's uncool with all these rich folks around there. I felt pretty embarrassed, I mean, I could have stood up tall and still walked under a closed door.

Everybody just busted out laughing and they were pointing at me. I was watching Jim. He didn't realize I was watching him and he turned around and faked a fall. Now we had all hit the ground a few times during the day and I knew he was sore because I was sore, too. And he wasn't a young chicken at that time. But Jim, he deliberately fell down and busted his butt just to make me feel not so bad. I watched him do it. He had to position himself just right in order to make it look real, and of course they all laughed and everything, but Jim just gets up and says, "See there, it can happen to anybody!"

When you get somebody like that, he makes you want to work harder, that is how he gets more out of you.

One afternoon, a fifth of Jack Daniel's and I sat down and I thought, "I'm going to write down thirty people that I'm not glad I met, but I'm honored to have met." I got through about eleven or twelve and realized two of them are working here in this building. One of them is Jim Frost and the other is Jeff Daniel. Truly, I have a set of standards that I couldn't meet, but these two people can and they were the ones that really started everything.

You go over to the children's hospital, and there is a quarter million dollars of special hospital beds that Jim put in there. He puts his money where his mouth is. I lived on 23rd Street when I grew up and he lived downtown as well. He started off selling watermelons. This guy has come a long way. He is more than blessed. These things are real. He is truly a good friend and he always has your back. He is a good teacher if you want to learn. I think he figured out some way, somehow, in some weird way, in some sequence of events, that if he gave something back he would be blessed. I know his mother, Margaret, is a good person. I think she instilled hard work in him, but so much of it he had to do on his own.

Jim is setting things up to go on and help the community, even after he is gone. This doesn't stop here, this goes on. He is going to leave his mark and it is a good mark. It is not one that is full of ego. You wouldn't believe how many churches, how many organizations, particularly if it has to do with youth, that he gives product to or cash right out of his pocket.

Let me give you another example. Jim had a ball team and they were playing in a World Tournament out west. The kids were very intimidated by the facilities, the stadium, the crowds, the really slick teams that were there. These were select groups of athletes, the best of the best of the best. One of the girl players told me that during a game Jim called a time out, gathered the team together in the outfield, and while everyone watched him, he went down on his belly and started eating the grass off the field. This freaked the girls out, freaked everybody else out, but Jim told his team, "We own this field, this is our field, they will not kick our butt on our field."

Of course it shocked them, but they got past the intimidation and it got them back in the ball game. Here is this multi-millionaire eating grass off the field to show them, "What are you afraid of? It is grass and dirt and sand, the same thing we play on back at home. I would never think to do that. I think that is what separates him from most people.

This is what I do in employment interviews. I do all the hiring and I tell potential employees if you feel like you have to steal something, talk to us and Jim will give you the knife. If you need money for gas to get home we will loan you the money; don't steal a knife and go and

sell it. Don't go there. You are going to need this job and you don't
want to go there. That blows some people's minds.

I believe by volume of product, do not quote me specifically on
this, but by number of pieces—pieces that go out of the building—I
think we are the world's largest distributor of cutlery. By total dollars,
I don't know, but by number of pieces that go out of here, we ship a lot
of product.

I think this is a success story for Jim and his family, which happens
to be about the cutlery business. I'm sure there are success stories all
over the country, but instead of driving Porsches and Maserati's and
all that other stuff, this man has given millions and millions of dollars
back to the community.

Describe your warehouse and shipping duties.

When I started here they had only a few phone sales operators.
Jim told me at one point that we would never have our own television
show, but tonight we will have thirty to forty-two phone operators
during the television show. If we can get the customers' orders out
fast, if they don't have any troubles, they reorder. The faster we get the
orders to the customer, the more impressed they are with our service.

What the customer sees when he gets his order and opens it up is
also very important. Sometimes I pull a box off the line, drop it on the
floor, throw it around, kick it, drop it from ten foot high and open it
up; just to see how the customer is going to get the knives inside. We
call this presentation, from the standpoint that, if the customer opens
up his box, even from the bottom, and see a Styrofoam mess or box
lids everywhere, then we have messed up. It looks unprofessional. I
check every knife and I feel confident that this guy is going to reorder,
because we delivered his order as promised. There is a certain honor
this business generally attracts. This is going to sound corny, but it
attracts people of honor. You don't last long in the knife business if
your word is not good.

Has Jim imparted any other words of wisdom upon you?

Jim Frost said something to me one time about twenty-four or twenty-five years ago. He said, "You give a man a knife with his name on it or you give a man a knife, he will remember you."

Now that doesn't necessarily mean he will like you, but he is going to know who you are for the rest of his life. I have given a lot of people knives; customers that might have a complaint, customers that do not have a complaint. Also we kind of make it a habit around here that most guests get a knife before they leave.

We've heard rumors that you and Mr. Frost are legendary practical jokers, and we've also heard a rumor about a joke that Mr. Frost played on you that actually involved a live goat. Is there any truth to such rumors?

Of course I'm innocent and pure as the driven snow when it comes to tricks and jokes and things of that nature! But that particular day was my birthday and normally I look for things from Jim and other people on that day.

Jim and I had gone downtown for some meeting and on the way back we stopped at a restaurant. The whole time we were eating we were talking business, and what I didn't realize was that Jim had actually taken my mind off the fact that it was my birthday. Normally on my birthday I'm always on my guard for Jim's practical jokes and always wondering what is coming. But with everything that was going on that day and the meeting downtown and the business talk over lunch at the restaurant, I lost track of the fact it was my birthday and I let my guard down.

When we got back to the office and I walked through the front door, I noticed that all the employees were gathered up front. So without thinking any more about it, I go over to my office and open the door—and there's a goat in my office! The goat jumps out of my chair onto the floor and stands there looking at me and bleating loudly.

Now Jim and I had been gone longer than we anticipated. I think that the goat had been in my office longer than anyone had ever expected. There were goat pellets all over my office. There were even goat pellets behind file cabinets! We haven't figured out yet how that goat managed to drop its pellets behind my file cabinets.

Jim Frost, left, pulling one of his practical jokes for Bob Johnston's birthday with a 'My Little Pony' ride. Johnston, right, said of this prank, "It's better than the goat any day."

Of course, when I turned around and looked, all the employees had gathered outside my door, and they all busted out laughing.

Was there any particular reason why a goat was chosen for this joke?

What you have to understand is that after I've been here at work for twenty-seven or twenty-eight hours straight. We've got a shower back in the back. There's an exercise room. I've eaten five meals here before I've left sometimes. I'll be saying, "I've got to get my goat-smellin' self out of here," and so I think that was part of it. That was the inspiration for the joke.

You both love practical jokes?

Occasionally I have been accused of pulling some [practical jokes], but those accusations are without merit. For example, I've been accused of sending employees to the back of the warehouse to find blade stretchers, or to go back to our trucks and take the winter air out of the tires and put the summer air back in them, and stuff of that nature. There's no proof of it.

But Jim loved playing this joke on me, and I think why he loved it was because he accomplished taking my mind off of knowing that this could happen.

Is there a "no harm, no foul" rule on your practical joking?

Well, you would have had to have been there to appreciate the goat, the odor. The odor was there. In fact, we had to redecorate my office. The little gal with the vacuum cleaner—one of those jet pack things—just kept vacuuming. Those goat pellets were everywhere. She said something to me once about when she cut the machine off and those pellets just went rolling back out the hose. I died laughing, because it was funny.

And of course, Jim, every day for three weeks, whenever he walked by he just busted out laughing. He didn't care that he spent ten thousand dollars redoing my office; he'd have done it even if it had cost him twenty-five thousand. He could have cared less because he loved doing it. Life at Frost Cutlery Company can be, from time to time, very colorful.

STACY COMBS
Combs Customs Knife Maker

Describe the Combs Customs knife line.

I make the custom knives for whoever and whatever, the "Combs Customs." I went in to see Jim a few years ago and told him I was going to start doing repairs to knives on the side. When I started taking the knives apart, I thought to myself, I might be able to do something with these. So I started filing them and doing bolster work on them. I had an idea and ran it by Jim and he said, "Let's put it on-air and see if it works."

It worked.

Usually if Jim wants to try something, nine times out of ten, it is going to work. Whatever he touches turns to gold. We hit the ground running with the Combs Customs and it has been going ever since. We didn't start airing them on the television show until December 2009, but I started training and practicing on them about two years prior.

There is a gentleman named Michael Prater who has a line of custom knives which are called Painted Pony. I have worked on the weekends helping him out when he didn't have enough people when he first started out. I would sit there and watch him, but other than that, no one else has been teaching me. My style is completely different from his; out of respect for him, I don't want to try and copy him.

I might do one of twenty-five of a Combs Custom Knife Set but each one is going to be different no matter what I do. Each will be a one-of-a-kind because I do each one by hand. I don't have any jigs, any diagrams to go by, everything is in my head. I will just freehand the designs. You will have one that will have a diamond up in the corner and on another one it will be a little further down or something similar. Even the file marks are not measured out, to where they are perfect on each one. Each one is one-of-a-kind Stacy Combs original.

What is your favorite knife to customize?

Stacy Combs working on a Combs Customs knife.

My favorite knife to customize is the Hen & Rooster. Any Hen & Rooster I love to take apart. I think German steel is ten times easier to work with than any other knife blade. You know you don't want to buy a generic brand of clay and an expensive brand of clay and two days from now the generic one is hard as a rock and the expensive one is just as soft as the day you bought it and easy to work with, that is the way I look at it.

Does Mr. Frost have a workstation next to yours in the warehouse?

Yes. What I do most of the time, is to turn up my music real loud so I can't hear him. If I'm working and I can hear Jim, I get up and turn up the music louder and go right back to work. Then he will get up and come over to me and say, "Hey can we do this?"

I will answer, "Leave me alone, I'm working."

I throw things at him, and he will throw stuff back at me. Practical jokes, picking on each other, there are no problems whatsoever with that. He will say to me, "Hey, what do you think about this right here?" and I will grab my earplugs, stick them in and go back to work.

LEE ROBERTSON
Frost Falcons Softball Organization/Assistant

Tell us about Jim Frost and the Frost Falcons.

I coach Frost's Falcons Softball and I remember all the things Jim did when he was coaching—the fun he had with the kids, how much fun he had coaching, the enthusiasm that he brought to the girls and to the game and how much he loved it. I use a lot of the same things he did twenty to twenty-five years ago and I try to apply it today to the things I do. Jim is a great motivator. He was a character when it came to the girls and keeping them excited about playing and motivating them.

Jim has been recognized for a lot of things he has done, but he doesn't do it just to get his name in the paper. I truly believe he does it for the kids. Not only in Chattanooga but from North Georgia to Knoxville, there are many people who have benefited from the things he has done.

The energy that Jim brings to Frost Cutlery day in and day out to the operations of the company is amazing. And the fact that somebody as successful as he is and still loves to be here is also amazing. Jim is definitely an inspiration to me and he does inspire people. He takes the time to let people know, "Hey, I appreciate what you are doing." You want to do well for Jim because he makes you feel that way. He gives you the praise and pats you on the back.

Jim surrounds himself with a good group of people that want to see the company succeed and want to see him succeed and can carry on even after he is gone. I believe Frost Cutlery will continue on because of what he's instilled in the employees.

I have faith in Jim and he has been an inspiration with the things he's taught me and still teaches me every day. Jim instills in you that you can never stop learning and he exemplifies that in his daily life. If there is somebody that knows more than he does about something, he is willing to listen to them and then apply it to his own business or to his own life. He is certainly somebody I look up to and admire.

RHONDA BOONE
Former Chief Executive Assistant

What are your duties at Frost Cutlery?

The main jobs I perform are in purchasing and developing of our product. I create the purchase orders with detail when ordering product. I manage and coordinate the emails with our foreign vendors overseas on a daily basis in working out the specifics of the product we order, checking on the status

Rhonda Boone and Jim Frost.

of the product and inquiring about new product. The emails are answered by Scott Combs and Jim, and I forward those answers on to the vendors. I stay in contact with our forwarding agent in shipping that product to us. I enter the product into our system and in receiving when it arrives here. I wire payment to some of the vendors. I also do payroll for Frost employees. That's just to name a few of my jobs.

Tell me about Jim Frost.

The first thing that comes to mind is that Mr. Frost is a workaholic. He likes to stay busy, he is always doing something. Sometimes you have to get his attention or make him focus, because his mind is somewhere else, he is on one track and you say, "I need you on this track for a moment."

I do remember him saying when we were in the last two buildings before this one, that he didn't want to get any bigger. But you get to a certain point and you run out of options. You have to move, expand and keep growing. He's one of those people that whatever he touches turns to gold.

He is funny too. He can be a jokester. I remember one time, when we were over in the other building and we had these cubicles. One of the ladies was on the phone. Mr. Frost thought he was going to be funny and swing his leg over her head. He didn't make it and he fell onto the floor. "Way to go Jim!" I told him. "I guess you won't be doing that ever again?" That was priceless!

He likes to laugh and to joke. He will say something and I tell him, "I'm worried about you . . . are you all right?" And he will say, "I get no respect around here." He's funny. Of course, he has his business side, too!

What is your proudest Frost Cutlery/Jim Frost moment?

I was behind the scenes for the building of the Jim Frost Stadium. Jim had me prepare letters to explain to people what he wanted to do for the community, and to ask them for their help. I sent letters out to hundreds of people, went down there and looked over things, and we took brick sales and imprinted the names of donors on the bricks and laid them in place. I am glad I was part of this effort to help the community.

I remember that Mr. Frost was surprised when they decided to actually name the stadium after him, because he truly never expected that. He had no idea about it until the night the stadium was dedicated to him. He was just doing it for the girls, the community, to get scholarships and to help those athletes.

JAN WATSON
Information-Technology Director

Where do you fit in the Frost Cutlery/Jim Frost story?

I have been fortunate to work with Jim Frost for the last twenty-two years. I was there when he bought his first computer for the company and helped design the computer software that is, for the most part, still in place today. I have seen many changes in the company over the past few years but find Jim Frost is the same savvy businessman today as he was twenty-two years ago.

It has taken me a few years to become accustomed to how Mr. Frost does business. To me it seems the formula for success is always changing; in my opinion he is always thinking outside the box. Mr. Frost comes up with the idea and we, the staff, are required to make it happen. Sometimes I think he expects the impossible but as I start working on the project I, too, can see the results and how much the company will be affected. He has a lot of respect and faith in his employees and believes that we can make his ideas come to fruition.

Mr. Frost knows how to do business and he is a wizard with numbers. I always try to be a step ahead of what I think Mr. Frost is going to do next. It is a pleasure to work with someone that is always moving forward in a positive manner and only looking back to see how he may improve his business for the future. I can honestly say that I have changed the way I think (no longer inside the box), to only see success and never let your mind be idle.

Are there any other key players in the Jim Frost story?

Jeff Daniel is a very important key person in this company. He is the glue that keeps everyone together. Jeff relates to everyone in the company, from Mr. Frost to the person that sweeps the floors in the warehouse. Jeff is a good listener. Many times I will discuss ideas or problems with him knowing that he will do his best to help me come to a resolution that best benefits the company.

Jan Watson and Jeff Daniel bouncing ideas off each other. Jan has a reputation throughout the company for always having her "ducks in a row."

Jeff has the best interest of everyone that works for Frost Cutlery. No one person does as much for Frost Cutlery as Jeff Daniel. He has the respect of everyone within the company; I don't know that you could find anyone that would say a harsh word about him. He has been with Mr. Frost for so long that he is an intricate part of Jim Frost and Frost Cutlery. He is a down-to-earth guy, and Jim Frost is lucky to have him as well. I think it has been a good relationship between the two.

MIKE SARRATORE
Corporate Account Salesman

What are a few of your job duties?

Basically I am a part-time salesman and part-time Jim Frost's personal assistant and handyman. The scope of my job entails everything from warehouse work and maintenance, to acquiring Jim's company and personal vehicles. I also spend a great deal of time tending to details of Jim's home and recreational vehicles, like the boats and jet skis, and winterize them

Mike Sarratore working at his desk.

every year. I tend to the needs of Jim's mother and home maintenance as well. You could say I keep the Frost family going from beginning to end, night and day, year-round. My job is secure for life because there is always something breaking somewhere, either at the warehouse or at Jim's house.

Over twenty years of working for Jim and with the company I have done numerous jobs. I worked in the Etching Department for a while doing knife customization. I rewired the deep etching machines. I purchased the laser etching machines and got those programs going so we could expand into that market.

One area in particular that is a great source of pride and enjoyment is working with Masonic Lodges across the country on customizing knives. Being a Master Mason myself and a Shriner, it's a great feeling knowing that you are working with an organization that does so much charity for communities across the country. I have been working with the Grand Lodge of Tennessee for more than twenty years, and in 2010 I was appointed the official Knife Maker of the Grand Lodge of Tennessee. I was honored and humbled by being given the title.

Jim Frost with NASCAR legend and dear friend, the late Dale Earnhardt Sr., in a photo taken by Jim's wife, Jan Frost. The two men are laughing because Jim had kissed Dale on the cheek just before this photo was taken.

I have to say that one of my proudest cutlery achievements was working on a Masonic knife campaign with Ed Jennings, who was the Grand Master of Georgia in 2009. The Masonic Children's Home in Macon, Georgia, was coming up short on funds. Ed took all the profits from his knife sales from his year as Grand Master and gave it to the Children's Home. I am not sure what the grand total was but I know at one point that he was able to donate over $50,000 to the Children's Home from knife sales alone. That act of charity could not have been accomplished if it wasn't for Frost Cutlery Company, and I am glad to say that we were a part of it.

Tell me about Frost Cutlery.

Frost Cutlery Company is a good organization. It's the biggest small business you'll ever see. We have come a long way and have many great employees and customers. I come from an Old Italian family, and much of what I have been taught can be applied to our company; you

Jim Frost with Richard Childress, left, former NASCAR driver and owner of the Richard Childress Racing team.

do right, you live right, you treat people right or you reap the costs. Frost Cutlery Company is only as good as the people it consists of, and so many of us have a piece of our lives invested in it.

Tell me about Jim Frost .

Jim Frost's mental talents amaze me. You can take just about any knife out of your pocket and show it to him and he can tell you where it is made, who made it, how much it cost to make, what a distributor should sell it for and how much a consumer is willing to pay for it. Jim knows knives and the knife market.

Jim is a numbers guys. If you look up the phrase "numbers guy" in a book, you will see Jim Frost's picture right there by the definition. He can crunch numbers in his head faster than any computer ever made by man. I guess that's part of Jim's mystique, because while everyone else in a meeting is sitting with their calculators, Jim is waiting for you to catch up so he can move on to the next thing. You had better have your ducks in a row when it comes to numbers and money, because

Jim is already two steps ahead of you the second you give him a number.

What sets Frost Cutlery Company apart from everybody else?

Even though we are a multimillion dollar company, we are still just a family business. No customer is too big that we can't handle, yet no customer's business is too little that we don't appreciate it, because it's the customers who keep us in business. It doesn't matter if you are a 4,000-store retail chain or a mom-and-pop store in a small town; you are going to be treated the same way, regardless. Even with the increased use of technology, we still haven't lost our personal touch. Jim started with a lunch box and now has a warehouse over 150,000 square feet; you don't have that kind of growth without treating people with respect and taking care of customers.

Still today, many agreements are done with a handshake. A man's word is everything here at Frost Cutlery Company. Our contracts with Richard Childress and Dale Earnhardt Sr. were all handshake agreements lasting over twenty years. There is a particular story I like to tell, about Jim and Dale Sr., that I was witness to a number of years ago. One day Jim and I were delivering Dale's royalty check to him. Unexpectedly, Dale pulls Jim and me into a meeting with some of his people. Dale says, pointing at Jim, "Look at this man right here! I never have to worry about him. If a royalty check is due today, he either brings it here personally or its next day aired to my desk. You never have to worry about Frost! All these people you signed up under contract pay late or don't pay at all!" I will never forget that day because it engrained in me even more that a man's word is his honor and his bond. Jim Frost's word has been the Golden Rule, for me personally and for the company.

At the end of the day, Frost Cutlery is a family. I've worked at other businesses before working for Jim. The day of my mother's funeral, my previous employer called me to see if I would come in to work but when I started working for Jim, it was much different. When my father was dying, during lunch I would go home and check on him. One day I went home during lunch and he had passed in his sleep. Jim couldn't have been more supportive. He said, "Mike, take all the time off you need, and let me know if there is anything I can do for you." You couldn't have a better friend and mentor.

We are intertwined in so many ways. Stefanie and Stephen and many of the employees, myself included, attended Tyner School. We knew each other as children and have grown up together. Now our children are growing up together. Time has bound us close to each other. It's something special and unique that you don't find in a lot of places. Frost Cutlery Company is not just a company; it's a family legacy that will span generations for years to come.

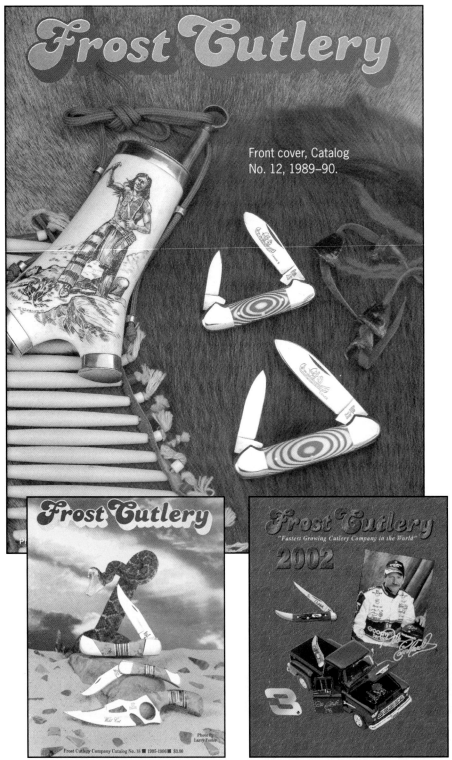

Front cover, Catalog No. 12, 1989–90.

Front cover, Catalog No. 18, 1995–96.

Front cover, Catalog No. 24, 2001–02.

TAMI WORLEN
Art Director

How did you come to Frost Cutlery?

Several years before I began working at Frost Cutlery, when I was in college, I was talking to Jim about the business, and was surprised to find out that he did not have an in-house design department. At that point, I was explaining to him the advantages of having a design department, and that the financial benefits would be tremendous. A big part of what Jim looks for is ways to economize things. So, when I

Tami Worlen in a creative moment.

explained how quickly he could recoup the investment of computers and software when considering having a designer available on a daily basis, rather than investing about $80 an hour for a per-job project, it really spoke to that aspect of his business sense. He did hire someone, sort of minimal, to do the custom knives, and do films and things like that. When I got out of college, this area of the business was beginning to grow, as was technology. When an opening came up, Jim asked me if I might be interested working for him in this capacity. The challenge and creative aspect of the job interested me; so, I jumped on it.

It has worked out well, because Jim likes to get things done, and I enjoy taking the initiative to get a project completed without a lot of supervision. He doesn't care about the process, but wants to see the final result fast. For example, last week Stacy Combs came into my office, and said, "This is one of my custom knives, and Jim wants an etch designed for it." I put it on the top of my priority list, since it was something that Jim wanted, but I did not expect a call from the Laser Department ten minutes later. Jim was there asking for the completed sample. So he can be very demanding in that respect.

The design department that I proposed to him years ago is now an integral part of the company. On a daily basis we will take photographs of products, create print and web advertisements, generate packaging for the manufactures, design new branding logos, and produce artwork for all of the in-house custom products. Custom orders have grown exponentially since we have acquired three laser machines and an imprinting machine. This necessitates that this department work closely with sales and production to make the orders efficient and ontime.

What is your favorite Jim Frost story?

Quite often when Jim is in a jovial mood, he will walk around the office sort of singing a tune. The song isn't really a song, but just a compilation of a few. It goes kind of like "Oh, have I told you laaaate-leee, mah darlin' . . . " So, one day, he is doing his little ditty, and gloating around, when he decides that he is Bruce Lee. He proceeds to make this belting "H-I-I-I-I-YAH!" sound and do a "karate kick." His foot hits one of the file holders that hang on the wall, and knocks it off.

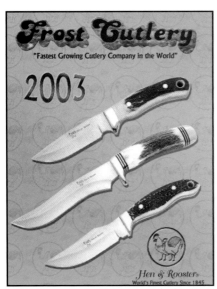

Front cover, Catalog No. 25, 2002–03.

Front cover, Catalog No. 26, 2003–04.

Then I see his feet over his head and his butt hit the ground. Everyone laughed, including Jim, for days after that. That is one thing you can say about Jim; no one laughs harder at themselves or their own jokes than he does.

He's very much a practical joker. Jim is a very generous man and he combines that with his humor. One day he walked by my and Camilla's office and said, "You guys do such a great job, I want to buy you lunch." So he gets in his pocket, he pulls out a $100 bill and rips it in half, and gives her one half and me one half. He gave us a hundred bucks, for lunch, but we had to go together, so it was a joke and his generosity all in one.

What are you proud of the most with Frost Cutlery?

I am proud to be a part of so many of the parts of marketing and product development in the company. Many times Jim will present a raw idea of something he knows will be a good product line or product, and I help to "polish" it. He came up with the idea of "Quality is a Family Tradition," for the then new Frost Family product line. I thought, "Well, if they are going to use the family crest, it might be nice to have that saying in another language." It ended up that *Qualitas est Familia Institutio* became the slogan for that product line.

Why Latin?

I thought it would be something that people would recognize, at least to some degree; that they could infer what it might mean, or perhaps be curious enough to look it up. The idea of tradition was in the back of my mind, and Latin is rich in history.

Michael "Shorty" Sherill
Customizing Shop Supervisor

Is the Custom Shop busy?

Busy is an understatement. It gets really hectic around Christmas. The Christmas rush is when a lot of the deep etching comes in, with a bunch of big companies ordering about 1,500 to 2,000 knives with deep etching. Those are all done by hand, every one. Most years we have to run two or more shifts to get the Christmas orders done.

Deep etching uses an acid saltwater bath with electricity, followed by cleaning and polishing, then painting?

Yes. We go through the deep etch, then we wipe them down after we dilute them in the salt, then we polish them and then paint them. It's a three step process. That means a 2,000 piece knife order turns into 6,000 individual hand processes, not including the reboxing.

Is any knife easier to engrave or deep etch over another?

The hardest two steels to etch are Hen & Rooster and W.R. Case. They take the longest time to etch. When deep etching with an acid saltwater solution, and if the steel is harder, it does take a little bit more time. I like working with the Hen & Rooster and Case better, because they take the deep etch better. With laser engraving it doesn't matter if it's China steel versus German steel or American steel; the burn time is all the same. As far as color painting the blades, they all take the paint the same.

What about the new Print Pad Machine?

Anything they can do on a computer the Art Department usually sends to us, or we can make the same images here in any color the customer desires. It goes back to that one-of-a-kind appeal. It has endless possibilities.

What is it like working with Jeff Daniel?

Mr. Daniel is really a good guy. I used to live real close to him. Sometimes he would come by at five o'clock in the morning to get his hair cut by a lady that lived down at the end of the road. He would always blow the horn to wake me up. He's always teasing me about being a morning person. We are always joking around with each other.

Jim is always pulling pranks and stuff like that, too. From day to day, it is a different comedy. It is a fun place. There is a time to play and a time for business, but then there is a time for both. You are busy but you can still have fun. Everyone knows which time it is.

What makes Frost Cutlery such a great place to work?

I have worked at some real crappy jobs but this place is like gold. I love working here. If I didn't, I wouldn't have been here for nine years. Every chance they get, Jim and Jeff take care of you.

Christmastime is the best time. It's unbelievable. Jim is in such a great mood, like he is Santa Claus. It is enjoyable coming in here, because every day he is pulling pranks. At times he has come through the warehouse singing at the top of his lungs. It is fun.

Jim is an excellent boss. Everybody here takes pride in what they do because we need to do our best for him, not only to make us look good, but to make him look good in order to keep his reputation. We are known all over the world. We have never missed a deadline, never. Everybody pulls together like a family, so instead of making everything difficult, it actually makes it not so bad.

The best part is, in most real big companies like this, the owners can't name everybody. I guarantee you Mr. Frost can go around and tell you everybody's first name, last name, middle initial, whatever. He's involved with the company. He actually cares about the people that work for him. It is the biggest satisfaction at the end of the day.

As I was leaving work on a Friday afternoon, I told Mr. Frost to have a nice weekend and he said, "I really do appreciate all the work you do for me, just remember that." That makes it worth it all.

GEORGE AMES
Corporate Accounts Manager

What do you do at Frost Cutlery?

I work with national accounts and large store groups, and I work on developing product lines that fit their needs.

Describe Private Labeling.

Private labeling is a common practice where a manufacturer or distributor will develop a product line under the name of a particular brand or retailer for sale to their customers.

Tell me about Jim Frost.

Jim has been a very successful businessman based on hard work, understanding his market and taking advantage of key opportunities in the market. Jim is very active in the business and understands the need for growth in new markets and changes in old markets.

He is what I would call a "deep thinker," and is always coming up with ideas to grow the business. He also does a lot of charitable work in the community and has helped a lot of people. My first experience with Jim was about twenty years ago. My son's baseball team needed a sponsor and one of the other parents said, "Call Jim Frost, he'll help us," the coach made one phone call and Jim sent a check for full sponsorship.

PATRICK SHIPLEY
Assistant Corporate Accounts Manager/
Marketing Coordinator/EDI Coordinator

What sets Frost Cutlery apart from other knife companies?

Frost Cutlery is one of the few knife companies that has survived the last few years of economic turmoil and continues to grow. Frost has been able to adapt, whereas many others have not, and so have gone the way of the dinosaur.

The defining element that makes Frost different than most other companies is product diversity. Frost Cutlery makes everything from swords to kitchen cutlery to pocket knives to hunting knives, and also the gift products and the coin collectibles. Not being locked into one genre of product means that if one product line goes soft, we shift our focus to another. It is our saving grace.

What kind of person is Jim Frost?

I will give you one of my Jim Frost stories. The 2009 season was the first year my daughter, Bianca, ever played softball. She was playing at the Middle Valley Park and was on one of the last teams that they put together. They were about a month behind on both practices and fund-raising. I went to Jim and explained it to him. He pretty much handed me all the money he had in his pocket, right then and there, to help her team. I'm not going to tell you the amount, but it was a good sum of cash. That's just the kind of guy he is—especially when it comes to helping children.

What is your role at Frost Cutlery?

It's not a role, but multiple roles. I don't know anyone in the company that works on the office side of things that has just one job. That's just not the Jim Frost way of running a company!

Just before I started, George Ames succeeded in getting a knife program in ACE Hardware. In order for us to grow the program and the sales, we needed to sell knife displays to as many stores as we could.

George and I sat down and he explained to me that we needed to develop a flyer, something short and to the point. The store buyers needed to be able to glance at a few bullet points about each product to be able to make a buying decision quickly, then have an easy order form to fill out and fax to us with their information.

Jay Haggard, left, and Jim Frost discuss a sword in the walk-in showroom area.

JAY HAGGARD
Corporate Sales/Softball Coordinator

What do you do at Frost Cutlery?

I started in the warehouse and Etching Department. A few years later I worked with the Sporting Goods accounts in the Corporate Accounts Division. I sold to the sporting goods chains, and I helped in the development of the hunting and fishing knives. After Jerry Lawhorn retired I took over the retail sales in the store. I also manage the Hen and Rooster website and direct the Hen and Rooster Collector's Club with Mike Sarratore and Patrick Shipley.

What are you most proud of at Frost Cutlery?

To be honest, the thing that I am the most proud of is that we do softball here. That is our thing. Jim has sponsored teams since 1983 and we have sent over 250 girls into college scholarships from our

Jay Haggard, back left, with a Frost Falcon team.

program. That is my biggest thing; I help run the Frost Falcon's Program, and I'm one of the coaches.

We basically coordinate the teams we have, monitor the kids, make sure where the people are playing and maintain the records. We like to stay in touch with all our different coaches. Our goal is to keep a different team in every age group and Jim sponsors that. We make the teams work.

Jim will give them knives to sell to raise money. The girls will go out and sell the knives. They can make great money off of them.

Instead of just giving them a free handout, they work for it. They have a lot more respect for themselves and what they get when they know they had to work for it.

The Frost Falcons program puts tens of thousands of dollars back into softball in this area. There is just so much that Jim has done for this community and probably ninety-eight percent of the people have no idea of what he has done, but he doesn't want the recognition.

The beautiful Warner Park facilities down by the Jim Frost Stadium at UTC-Chattanooga are mainly used for the upper level of competitive softball. Last year we started the Jim Frost Memorial Day Classic softball tournament, a tournament for the recreational kids.

Normally these kids would never get the opportunity to play at a place this beautiful like this park. We were expecting to get a few fields to do this tournament and we ended up with about sixty teams. The tournament not only used all five fields, but the stadium, too. Kids who had never even been in this park all of a sudden were walking out onto those fields. Jim said, "The look on those kid's faces was worth every dime we put into it." Those kids walked out from the dugouts and you could literally see tears in their eyes.

The money that we made off of that tournament, which was a minimal fee, we turned it right back into a scholarship for softball players who don't receive college scholarships.

I don't believe softball would have been as big in this area as it is if Jim hadn't started that first little "Switchblade" Team. If it wasn't for Jim, I know Chattanooga wouldn't be the Mecca it is today for fastpitch softball.

We did another little tournament last year. It was one of those little bitty fun ones where the teams pay the umpires. Jim was down there watching softball when one of the umpires came up to me and said, "Hey, those teams over here don't have the money to pay me, what do you want me to do?"

I said, "I'll take care of it."

I turned around and Jim reached in his pocket and gave her $60. That is just the way he is.

Phil Martin
Owner, Blue Ridge Knives

How did you meet Jim Frost?

I met him when he was in business with Jim Parker. That is when I first got to know him. One of the things I like to remember about Jim is that when he started out on his own he worked out of his house. I was working the shows, had a van and traveled the roads. I would come by Jim's house and he would raise his garage door and that was his office and he had his inventory in there. I would back my van up to his garage and we did business in the garage. Then I would go on to a show. Later on he got a building and hired Jeff Daniel, and Jeff is still with him after all these years.

My business grew along with Jim's business. He was always really fair and he always did what he said he was going to do. It was easy. There wasn't any negotiation. This is the deal and he always left you room for your profit. He was fair to do business with. If you had a problem, you could call him up and talk to him about it and he would fix it. Jim is successful because of his ideas in developing product for the market and bringing unique items to the market that nobody else has and doing a good job with that. People look to Frost because of all these different brands he has, like his Hen & Rooster brand or his Buck Creek brand. He makes himself stand out differently from everybody else and that is what makes people want his product.

Jim was always trying to help me. He always said, "What can I do to help you grow your business? What can I do to help you personally?" He was always there for me.

The one thing that impressed me the most is when one of my competitors retired and sold out his company. I was interested in purchasing the company, but I didn't buy it; someone offered more for it than I was willing to pay. One day I was having lunch with the company's owner and he said to me, "One of the things that I think your company Blue Ridge Knives did better than my company,

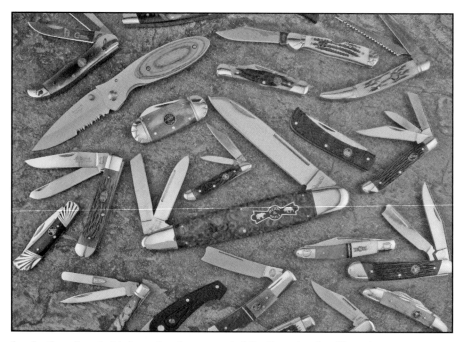

A selection of pocket knives showing several of the Frost family of brands.

something that helped set you apart from other knife companies, was your relationship with Frost Cutlery and with Jim Frost." It was a very impressive statement. This guy had never handled Frost knives, and yet for years he had felt that we had always done such a nice job with Frost's knives and that was the reason why we had always out-competed him in the market. That really stood out to me because he didn't have to say anything at all.

What has been your experience with Jeff Daniel?

Jeff is always a real straight, honorable guy, just like Jim Frost. You could call him and he would always take your call. If he didn't know the answer you needed he would get you the answer. I remember when he started working for Frost. You could always depend on him and for him to tell you the truth and also for him to tell you what he thought. He is a very dependable fellow. I mean, if you wanted to ask somebody something about Frost, if you couldn't talk to Jim then you talked to Jeff. I have a lot of respect for Jeff, because of what he has always done.

CHAPTER 3

The Cable Show

A FTER A DECADE OF SUCCESS and growth in wholesale, most entrepreneurs would have been content to ride the wave of success in to early retirement. An enduring legacy and a secure customer base were all but guaranteed for the long term. But the main character of our story isn't any other businessman who is satisfied with sustaining or maintaining the status quo. Finding and seizing opportunities are the essence of who he is as a businessman and as a leader. To ignore any potential is very contrary to his nature and one of the biggest prospects for development soon came in to his sights, despite his repeated protests, "I don't want to get any bigger."

Most of what the public believes about Frost Cutlery Company and its origins in the television market are myth mixed random facts in a jumbled timeline. To understand the picture of this patchwork of personal accounts and stories, it's best we take a moment to sharpen our image. In the late 1980's, Frost Cutlery products hit the airwaves with the assistance of Bruce Voyles. Dabbling here and there with different products and honing techniques, the eventual formulas for successful programming laid the groundwork for what was yet to come. In February 1996, Frost Cutlery products would soon be found on the Shop at Home Network. Shortly thereafter, in June of 1998, Home Shopping Network would feature Frost Cutlery products as well. Business was booming, products were flying off the shelf and into the homes of consumers.

After many years, Mr. Frost—unrelenting in his passion to move the business forward—took one of the biggest gambles of his career by starting his own television network and program. In September 2003 the Cutlery Corner Network (CCN) was founded. Starting out in studios in Dandridge, Tennessee, nearly two hours away from Frost

Cutlery Company headquarters, the first *Cutlery Corner Network* television show took to the air with great success.

As the years went by, faced with the ebb and flow of viewership, shrinking attention spans, advancements in technology as well as rising costs, the need for more control and the flexibility to respond even more quickly to the demands of a live audience forced the next step in the evolution of CCN. After months of planning, budgeting and development, the company's new Frost Media studios were built in the back of the warehouse expansion in Ooltewah, Tennessee.

Finally, in 2010, during the week of the Fourth of July, the *Cutlery Corner Network* television show went live from the new studios for the first time, under the direction and supervision of Frost Media employees and staff. Decades of hard-won experience, gained through trial and error, had come together to form the nexus for the finest, most well-developed program that viewers had ever seen to date.

TERRY DUNCAN
Cable Show/Product Sales Manager

How do you pick the knives to sell on the cable show?

It started with Todd [Boone, co-host of *Cutlery Corner Network*] who pulled me into this. He used to have to travel down twice a week from Knoxville to the Frost Cutlery warehouse and he would build some sets and I would help him, because I knew where almost everything was.

You can hand me any knife and I can

Terry Duncan examining a Steel Warrior pattern.

remember everything in our warehouse that had that particular knife in the set. A few years later, after we started into the network business and I got to be good friends with the show hosts, they requested that I help them get things together. On average I get about sixty phone calls a day about the knives from within our headquarters or from other companies: "Hey Terry, what was the CCN number for that set?" and "What about the Blue Bone Trapper that was on-air this weekend?"

This is what Frost saw in me. One day he walked through the warehouse and asked, "Where are the little Warriors?"

I told him, "It's back there on shelf location B-217."

I guess I have somewhat of a photographic memory for our item numbers and the places they are at in the warehouse. Not just the number, but if you give me the name of the knife, what it looks like and an idea of what it is, I know any knife that we have.

How does the show work?

Todd shows up a couple of hours before the show and gets the entire product ready. Todd knows what he wants to sell on TV. He will be on-air and Mr. Frost will send him a picture of a big old fish or something to Todd's cell phone. Todd will look at it and put it on-air.

You will see the energy behind a two-hour block of the live show. It is a constant talking to the cameras, a constant shuffling of product, knowing what is what and where everything is and going to be.

Todd is a pro, the best in the business. He has a following out there, he has been doing it for many years.

Where does Tom O'Dell fit in the show?

Tom is a nut and Todd is serious. When they first started [*Cutlery Corner Network*] it was a comedy show. It was like *Saturday Night Live* and they all had fun. Tom O'Dell has been on the *Jimmy Kimmel Show*, because Kimmel is a big fan of Tom O'Dell. My eight-year-old son Seth has been on-air several times. My son says Tom O'Dell is his first best friend. Tom O'Dell and he are like big buddies. Tom would chase him out in the yard of the studio. Tom put him on-air near Christmastime and Tom was holding him in his arms asking him what he wanted for Christmas. It was great for the show and people really liked it.

What's it like having the show in the back of the building instead of two hours away?

One word: awesome. It's the first time in fifteen years I have been in town on a Friday night. Having the studio in the building allows us to do things we never could before. It allows us to show more product, more prep time and be able to respond quickly to the demand for certain products on the show. The unlimited access to the product in the warehouse has been completely awesome. Plus now that we are using our own production crew, training our people the way we want the show done and how we do things makes us more efficient. The costs savings alone will benefit our customers because we can pass those savings along to them.

Did you ever think the company would ever have its own studio?

Yes, without a doubt. If you think about it, all the show has ever done is grow over time. As it grew in size, so did the costs of doing it. Building the studio was just a logical progression in the growing process.

What influence do you have on the studio?

All my influence for the show is always behind the scenes. I give my advice on how the show should be run and the setup of the products, etc. What our producers and crew do with that advice is at their discretion. I just want the show to work and to sell the most products we can on any given night. It's not about who gets the credit but about doing what's best for the show and what works.

What is your relationship with Jim Frost?

I consider Jim Frost to be my second father. I treat him like my dad. I am a 23-year employee. I started as a warehouse worker and now I am a Product Sales Manager and Product Buyer. I wouldn't be where I am now if it wasn't for Jim Frost. I owe him so much for all the blessings in my life.

What impresses you the most about Jim Frost?

I used to attend meetings with Jim at HSN, Shop at Home, etc. I sat and listened like a fly on the wall most times. Many of the people in the room had college degrees, master's degrees and all this experience in business. Jim could stand toe-to-toe and surpassed many of them. He is such a savvy businessman with such a keen wit and intelligence that he earned and acquired from all the years of doing business. In all our dealings, Jim's concern was always looking out for what was best for the customer when preparing for a show. Most employees can't say that about their boss.

Anything else you would like to add?

The quality of the knives has always been good, but it has gotten even better over the years. I attribute this to Mr. Frost and he gets full credit. Mr. Frost's buying ability is unbelievable and he is by far one of the best buyers in the marketplace. He is phenomenal when it comes to getting in there and making the deal and demanding the quality. He has improved the quality of the knives and lowered the costs of our products. If you look back on shows from years past, not only have we lowered the cost of the product to us, but we lowered the cost to the consumers. No one else really does that.

Mr. Frost's brain is constantly thinking up new ideas. The first thing he does is tell one of us and he wants it done right away, then it is off his mind. It is amazing all the stuff he has come up with over the years. When my son visits Frost Cutlery, of all the people in that building, the first person he wants to see is Mr. Frost. I don't know if it is the energy he puts out, but he gives motivation to young people extremely well and they pick up on it.

Jeff Daniel is one of the most incredible people I have ever met in my life. I respect Jeff. What Frost did was he started Jeff out when he was just a kid, working out of his garage. When I think of Frost Cutlery, Jeff Daniel is one of the first names that come into my mind. He is our VP and everybody likes Jeff and you can't ask for a better man to show what our company is all about. He is the image that all of us would like to be. Jeff is the perfect employee for Mr. Frost.

TOM O'DELL
Cable Show Host/Salesman

Did you have the first knife show on satellite?

No, there was a knife show before us on satellite and it was the guy who does Blade magazine. He had a knife show, but we were definitely the first on cable.

Shop at Home Network started with humble roots in Newport, Tennessee. I started with them in 1989. Actually, I started working for Joe [the former show's studio owner] in 1984 but that is another story altogether. We moved to Knoxville in 1991 and that is where Todd and I did our first show in April of 1991. The guy selling knives did mostly antiques. No one had ever done what we did by offering a grouping of knives, so they let Todd and I have a shot at it.

Todd Boone was with Star Sales at the time and I wasn't even supposed to do the show with him. Another old boy was supposed to do the show but, in a strange turn of events, it turned out that I was the only one "country" enough to sell knives. That was their take on it.

It has been a steady rise and I have seen a lot of changes. I miss my old buddy Rex Bernard, the one that really helped us out. He was in the trio. We all started at Shop at Home. I trained Rex and Todd to do on-air, because I had done it a couple of years. Todd supplied the product at the time and then we brought Frost in. Honestly, the first couple of years, Todd and I looked at each other and said, "There's no way, we will be out of a job in a year." I think we all fell into this. It really wasn't a planned thing.

The fact is Todd wanted to bring in Frost. I give Todd tons of credit for that. It was his direction and I just followed suit. It has made a livelihood for me.

Tell us about Jim Frost.

All I can say about Jim is that he is an extremely smart and cunning man who is a negotiation wizard. He has to be a negotiation wizard to come up with the products we are able to sell on this TV network and at the prices we are able to sell them. Other companies making anything to look anywhere similar to his knives are $25 and we are selling them for $5 to $6.

Cutlery Corner Network host Tom O'Dell, left, being honored by Jim Frost on-air on Tom's birthday.

I think that Jim is the king of negotiation, period. He is probably the smartest businessman I have ever met and I have met a lot of them. Most of them had years and years of schooling and knew nothing about reality. Jim started from the ground up, out of his garage, right out of the trunk, his lunch box, the whole nine yards.

Jim is all about building a quality knife at an affordable price. Funny story to tell you: I had no idea who Jim Frost even was. I just barely knew what a knife was. So Todd comes up and I always said, "Jim's Bear Hunter Line, they are a dang good knife." At that time, everyone considered Pakistan knives junk. My words were, "They are a dang good knife for a piece of crap."

In the beginning Todd played a trick on me. He brings Jim in one evening and I had no clue who Jim was at the time; I had never met the man in my life. Todd said, "Tom, tell this man what you think about those Bear Hunters."

I said, "They are a dang good knife for a piece of crap."

Jim's eyes got about big around as softballs and he looked at me real funny like and Todd said, "I want to introduce you to Jim Frost the man that made those pieces of crap!"

Presumably, the relationship did get better, didn't it?

Jim laughed and he understood what I meant. It was hard to sell at that time. On-air it was really hard to sell anything that wasn't Case

XX or German. If it said "Japan" it was out. If it said "China" it was out. If it said anything other than "USA" it was out.

We introduced the world to Jim's knives. Comparing a Frost Cutlery knife to a Case knife, clearly it wasn't a Case knife, but it wasn't anywhere near the price of a Case knife either. My explanation was just that simple. The price was phenomenal for the knife as it was. It was a great knife. Dollar for dollar, you can't buy more. Here in Tennessee everyone is Case knife oriented. If it is not a Case knife, most people around here were really hesitant to buy it.

There was so much response [to the TV show] in the beginning . . . it was phenomenal. Rex really introduced us to cable. He was the best I have ever seen on any network. They wouldn't even allow Todd and me to go on cable to start with. They said we were "too country to be presented" on the cable network; seriously. But Rex fell in love with us, two hick rednecks, and so he wanted to try selling knives on cable.

Currently, we are doing as many as 175 different products in a show, versus the old days, when for a three to four hour show we had twenty items. Volume-wise we are showing a great deal more now. "If we are not showing you something at this moment that you like, hey, stick around with us, we are like the weather here in Tennessee, we will show you something different in just a second!"

What can you say about your co-host, Todd Boone?

I can remember when Todd, Rex and I all got to work together and we planned skits to perform on-air just to get people's attention. One New Year's Eve, we decided that we were all going to dress up. I dressed up as Father Time, Rex dressed up as Mother Nature and Todd dressed up as Baby New Year. Then we went on-air. I could blackmail Todd for years to come; we put him in a diaper! Rex, of course, had a dress on and he made a decent looking lady. I was Father Time and I just looked as rough as I normally do. I don't know if it actually helped sales, any of our gimmicks, but I know one thing; we kept people watching and that is a key to sales. If you can't keep them entertained they won't stick around. When we first started out, we had a lot of time to kill, because we were only showing twenty products in a four-hour period and you might talk thirty minutes about one item. Well, after the first five minutes the rest is fluff anyway because you told them the facts about the product or knife, so you are just filling in so it gave us room to do a lot of things. It really brought in a large crowd of viewers.

If they are watching, we will eventually show them something they want to buy. We had to do our dog and pony show just to get people to watch us. They would think to themselves, you all are regular people after all. We brought our personal life in it. My grandkids, I have always brought them in on their birthdays, you know, to get a camera shot of them. I think it helps a lot to let people know we are actually human.

What about Sheila Travis?

She is sweet, she really is. She is my right arm. The thing I hate the most is doing run sheets, doing paperwork, and she does the paperwork. She does the run sheet. I just tell her what I want on the run sheet and she selects the rest and what she wants to show on TV. It has worked out really well. Over the years I have worked with a lot of people and found out a long time ago that I like working with women. I love to joke around. I try not to take it too far, but sometimes it does go there.

I don't know if you have heard this story. We had a Buck Creek/Buffalo Creek Knife. It has one blade of each in the knife and it has both shields on it. I'm up there and cracked on her eight times in the last hour, so she is very wary about saying much. She gets up and she is going to do this knife—it is called a Buck Creek/Buffalo Creek Knife—and somehow it comes out as "Butt Crack." This came from Sheila, not me. You have to realize, she's from a news background and mistakes just don't happen. She's usually polished and professional even when I'm not.

Sheila is a great friend and she's got a great sense of humor. She and I have never had any cross words whatsoever. I'm lost without her. She is my right hand and I think we are better together.

SHEILA TRAVIS
Cable Show Producer/Host

What duties do you perform as producer of **Cutlery Corner Network?**

That means I select the knives, I put the sets in order. There is really an art to it. You really have to have so many items within that hour to make the dollars that Jim wants to make as far as your price points. You need to have the Large Set of course. It would be nice to have a Sword Set and then a mix of the Bowies, or the Tacticals and the Pocketknives, before the Speed Run. Jim likes to have a lot of different sets each night. When Todd gets done picking his stuff I look at what he has left and then I will go back to the cage and select the items for my show.

Cultery Corner Network producer and co-host Sheila Travis, right, with Jim's wife Jan Frost, in the CCN studio.

Will you use anything that Todd has shown in his earlier show?

Yeah, some of the new items that I really like that will be hot tonight and that people will buy.

Do you get feedback on how well an item is selling and how the show is running?

Yes. I do wear an IFB [Interruptible Feedback, worn as an earpiece] because I like to know what is going across the air. These guys don't know it, but a lot of times, it is kind of my way of controlling Tom [laughing], because he doesn't know when his microphone is on or off. He may walk out the door and be talking up a storm with somebody off set. I will have to turn my mike off and yell, "Turn his mike off!"

No matter how well you plan, produce or put together a show, it is

121

Pictured from left: Todd Boone, Jim Frost, Sheila Travis and Tom O'Dell, on-air talent for the *Cutlery Corner Network* television show on Frost Cutlery's Cutlery Corner Network.

going to change before the night is out. I come from a television news background—world of Teleprompters where everything has to be very accurate and factual. When I first came up here, I thought, "What are these guys talking about? Where are they getting all this info?" They were just rattling stuff off and it was all new to me. I'd never worked in an ad lib world before, but here we make it up as we go along.

Does Mr. Frost give you and your two co-hosts plenty of accolades?

He does a great job when he comes on the show. He's energetic, alive and crazy. You would not think somebody of his "Jim Frost status" would be like that. Jim sets a really high standard. I think everybody works really hard to meet that standard. Often it is because he is in the warehouse working; Jim is so "hands-on." I think if he was one of those stuffy guys sitting in his office doing nothing that people would not feel that way. He's such a team player.

TODD BOONE
Cable Show Host/Salesman

What can you tell us about the early days of the show?

When I went to do my first show, Tom was not scheduled to do the show with me. He was not ever considered to sell knives. A guy named Tommy was scheduled to do the show with me and I had never been on television, ever. So I was already nervous. I get to the studio and they told me to get there two hours early. This is Shop at Home when they were in Knoxville.

So I get there two hours early. I'm serious now, really nervous and scared to death. As soon as I get there, I had to check in at the guard shack. The lady that was over my knife category came out and told me that Tommy had been fired that day. I had previously come to the company, met Tommy, showed him the product and put in all this work training Tommy, and soon as I get there I am told he has been fired.

At first I thought I wasn't going to have a show but they said, we will put you with Tom O'Dell. Never seen Tom O'Dell, didn't know Tom O'Dell, wouldn't have known him if he was standing next to me.

Tom shows up five minutes before my live show starts. I was beside myself. I didn't know how Tom worked and he had very little air time experience. He was comfortable in front of the camera, but I could sense that he was also nervous because this was a category that he knew they really wanted to succeed.

I could see the pressure in Tom's face. It didn't help me either and that made it a lot worse for me. I didn't know what camera to look at, I didn't know that they had a review monitor and nobody told me anything about anything. Tommy was supposed to have done all that in the studio and rehearsed on what to expect and how it works before the cameras. At Shop at Home they had four cameras and two preview monitors. I knew nothing and was thrown in there and just did it. We sold $2,000 worth of product, which was not good.

They made me a tape of the show. I took it home and watched it and I realized everything I did wrong. On the second show I had people tell me that they didn't even know it was the same person. It was a completely different show and it was a lot better. That is what started it off. Tom would have never been in this business, if not for the day that Tommy got fired.

I have been through the thick and thin of all of this. I have been with all kinds of people. I have been with CEO's and all of those people that tried to tell me that I was not doing it right, that I needed to do something different and my time was limited. They are all gone and Tom and I are still here. I took bits and pieces that other show hosts have taught me. But as far as all the big wheels in all these other places that try to change the way we do it, we learned real quick what works and almost twenty years later we are still here. Big wheels, big talking executives, they are gone and are doing something else. Most of them are not in television, because this is not your typical retail type business. You can't treat it like retail business.

There are people that get hired in by these companies, Home Shopping Network, Shop NBC or Shop at Home, and they have these mile-long resumes and all of this experience with retail and that's great. But the television angle is completely different. All these years, I just remember it doesn't matter what their names are, they come in and it doesn't work. They don't last because this is not really retail. It is to a certain extent, but you can't go about what we do under any type of typical or traditional retail type format.

It used to be a lot different. We used to do a great deal of very low quantity items until we found the sets, the package sets. The multiple knife type sets that we do now is not the way the show started, it started with a lot of one-only type items and very expensive knives. We used to set the knives up ourselves and that was one of the reasons we were limited to how much product that we could show.

I used to set most of the knives up while I was on-air. People thought I had all kinds of people helping me. A gentleman came up to me one day at Home Shopping Network and said, "That was the number one pitch that I have ever seen on television." Our knife pitches, the way we did it, what I never told anybody, it really wasn't a pitch. We had to do it that way because we didn't have anyone to help set up our knife sets. For example, if we had a 15-piece knife set, I would only set up one or two knives and the entire pitch was us adding knives and dropping the price on the TV screen. If we were going to sell a $100 pocketknife set with fifteen knives in it, we would start at $200 and only have four knives on the table. Then we would drop the price $25 and add two more knives. People thought that this was a pitch. I guess to an extent it was a sales pitch, but more so than anything we didn't have a choice. We had nobody to set our product up, it worked out and we got lucky that it worked.

Currently, in a two-hour period, before I know it, I have shown a hundred items and I'm done. This is kind of difficult to do to be honest with you, because you are relying so much on your crew. It is not difficult for me; it is difficult for the crew.

The crews can make or break your shows. There has been many a show that we have lost thousands of dollars over a crew. Home Shopping Network had a couple of crews that were excellent, you couldn't ask for anything more. At Shop at Home it was more difficult there, because there was such a high turnover. We need people that start doing our show, and stay with it and learn it. Now I have crew members that know what I want before I say it.

Did Tom tell you what our first studio was like? The first show I did with him? The studio was about the size of a bathroom. It was not meant to be a studio, it was an office. We moved tables in and out of a regular size door, a door that you open up to go into an office. With tables of knives sitting in a hallway, it was a fire hazard. We always did what we had to do to get it done.

When I went to Home Shopping Network and worked with those people to get a show, Frost didn't know about it. I never told him. He had no idea. I gave up sixteen live hours a week, not counting the taped hours with Shop at Home, to go to Home Shopping Network in Clearwater, Florida. You know how much time they gave me for my first show? Eight minutes. I gave it all up for eight minutes, because I knew that I could do it. I knew that the product would sell.

I didn't take Frost knives, I took somebody else's. Like I said, Frost had no idea. I knew the product would sell. I knew in my mind that Shop at Home had 60-65 million full- and part-time viewers and most of those homes were in the middle of the night. I knew going in that Home Shopping Network had 87 million full-time viewers and that the only reason it wouldn't work was because of me. I gave it all up for eight minutes, but eight minutes turned into thirty, thirty minutes turned into an hour, an hour turned into two hours.

In those first eight minutes I aired three items. The first item was $22 and I sold 290 units in maybe two and a half minutes. Had an $89 item next that we sold 100, and the last item, a pocketknife set, was also in the $80 range. It was short-timed; I had about one minute on it and we still sold sixty of them. All in all, for such items with such a brief airing and nobody knew we were going to be there, it was a success.

We ended up getting more orders after my airing was over. More orders kept coming in throughout the day. This led to Home Shopping Network considering it as a viable category for selling on TV and they approved it for more air time.

After that first show, I realized that when I got back, I would have to go talk to Mr. Frost. I dreaded it, because I was hoping that he wouldn't think that I abandoned him, that I just threw him off to the side and did this on my own. I could have; I had other people's product. If I would have told Jim Frost beforehand what I was doing it would never have happened. He would have talked me out of trying it. We were new to all of this. We had a solid show, three to four nights a week at Shop at Home. We were a major vendor at that network and I put a wrench in it, bad.

I had some shows during the day at Shop at Home and they had 60 million full- and part-time viewers, most at two o'clock in the morning. I had Sunday afternoon shows at Shop at Home, but we probably had only around 20 million people watching. Home Shopping Network had from 87 to 88 million full-time viewers. That means at any given time of the day that you have a show, you have access to 88 million people that can watch you. There is no comparison. Big difference having that type of coverage and it did not require me to have to do shows every single week. I could sell more product in two hours at HSN than I could in two or three weeks at Shop at Home.

There was also a sister network in the same building, a smaller network they called America's Store. I would move out leftovers, low quantity items. Most times I would do a two-hour show and as soon as I would get done with that show I would go over to America's Store and do two more hours. I did that twice a month.

It got to where I was going to Florida every week. I ended up getting a Friday night show after a month or two, and people knew we were going to be on-air at this particular time at night. It took me thirty minutes to get to the airport in Chattanooga, hopped on the plane, flew thirty minutes to Atlanta, spent about another hour in Atlanta and hopped another plane and got down to Florida in about an hour. In about three hours I would be in Florida.

I did the first show with another company's product. The other company was not going to be able to handle this type of volume and it overwhelmed him. I used it as leverage for bringing Frost to HSN and after that first show I used Jim Frost and his company as leverage to get more time out of Home Shopping Network. Basically I told HSN that if they liked the results of the eight-minute airing, "We can do this and can make this work." Then I told them, "I can't do this in only 30-minute shows; I need to do more than that, and I will bring Frost Cutlery to you." And they said, "Okay."

Frost was already set up to handle the business. He could drop ship the product and knew what he was doing. Jim had all the keys and they just had to be turned. I only did one or two shows that were an hour and then it immediately went to two hours, two-hour blocks.

How long did your time in Florida last?

From eight minutes to seven years at Home Shopping Network is something I'm proud of. After four or five years, Frost and I were seasoned into it. At that point we knew what we were doing. We knew that this wasn't just a fly-by-night show and that it was here to stay.

The management changes at Home Shopping Network were brutal.

They were horrendous. Just as quick as you got the show going well, when you were set and everything was working smoothly, there would be management changes. They would just throw a wrench into the whole thing. There were several of these moments. The last one I went through, I had the feeling that we needed to do something, and with all the ups and downs and uncertainties that go with these networks, even after four and five and six years, you never knew what could happen.

I saw some major changes that were coming at HSN. I was walking down the beach in Clearwater with Frost one morning after a show, and I told him, "We have to do something and start the Cutlery Corner Network on our own. We are going to have to take this step or we are

The set of the *Cutlery Corner Network* television show in the Cutlery Corner Network studio.

going to wake up one day and have an e-mail saying that we don't have a show anymore."

Seven years earlier, when I got my foot in the door, they were adding male oriented products to the shows. They went for years doing the female type stuff and they needed to spice it up. They started adding male product categories, like sports cards, football shows, knife shows, tool shows and things like that. We went through that phase and it died out. I saw it coming, and as we walked down the beach and talked, Mr. Frost said, "Okay."

That is all he had to say, we did all the rest and we started working on a place, a person and a studio. After all those years with HSN I had learned how a major player does it. It was real important for me to do that; I know that now. There are still things I learn, but as far as the oranges and apples of all of it, I know that. "At nine o'clock it is air time, it is nine o'clock, it is nine o'clock!" That is what we used to say, and still do sometimes. There is no, "Hey wait just a minute." There is no stopping, no pausing, and no waiting a minute. It is nine o'clock and you are on, you are live, go with what you have, do the best you can with it. It doesn't stop, there is not a pause button, no stopping and saying, "Hey lets redo this." When you are live, you're live.

How did Rex Bernard figure into all of this?

If it hadn't been for Rex Bernard, I don't know that I would be where I am at today. I learned so much from that man.

Just to tell you how other people in the business thought of Jim Frost, Rex made a plaque for Jim that says, "Jim Frost is smarter than me, Rex Bernard." I have never seen anything like that done before. "Jim Frost is smarter than me . . . "

Rex was a walking dictionary or encyclopedia. Unbelievable; it was beyond amazing. Ask Rex about sixteenth century Japan and you would have to shut him up.

Where does Terry Duncan fit into the picture?

Terry is a good one. I have known Terry since way before we started doing any network shows. I met Jim and Terry when I started out as a part-time employee at Cutlery World. Terry is as good as they get and Terry is my best friend in this business. There is nothing I can't talk to him about; we click. He can get product in, or something new, and he knows whether I'm going to like it or not. It works that way. I have had arguments with Terry and the next day we go fishing. Business is business and friends are friends. It doesn't affect our relationship.

Terry and I did most of the work at HSN. A big portion of the meetings were meetings about meetings. We were stuck; thrown amongst the sharks is what we used to say about those meetings. I don't know what I would have done if Terry had not been there. Terry would sub for me if I couldn't do the shows, if I was off on vacation or something came up, Terry would do them on America's Store.

We had really good and bad times in Florida. Like I said, I don't know how I would act if Terry wasn't there to do what he does. I don't have to worry about that part of what Terry does; he is there, I know he can take care of it. I know right now Terry is working on product for tomorrow and this weekend. I used to go to Frost Cutlery's warehouse every week and select product for the show and it is such a great relief I am not forced to have that burden on my shoulders anymore. Now it clicks like a well-oiled machine.

We have a solid crew. The crew is the bloodline between me and the viewer. It has to look good. You can't have fingerprints, or a dirty turntable; the little things are important. I don't have to worry or think about that anymore because they are going to do it. I don't have to stop and turn off my microphone to tell them something. I have to turn off my microphone off less right now than any time in the history of doing this show. You don't want to have to turn your microphone off; if you turn your microphone off you can't sell anything. You don't want to do that. Now I have shows that I never have to turn it off.

What would you like people to know about Jim Frost?

Jim Frost is—and I'm not just saying this; I would say this tomorrow to anybody—he is almost like a father to me. Seriously, I have never met a person that I felt so close to—I don't want to get mushy—yet respected more than any person that has ever come into my life and I'm not talking about my family.

Jim is unbelievable when it comes to business, just unbelievable. He comes up with things that I just say, "Jim, come on man; let's not do that," and it works. That just tells me that I don't know everything. Hare-brained ideas, then it works, proves he is a genius at marketing.

Jim is a very shrewd businessperson. I can talk to Jim Frost about business and tell him an idea that I have and I never have to bring it up again. I have absolute, one hundred percent confidence that he has thought about the conversation we had about my idea and decided to do it or not. I never have to go back and ask, "Hey do you remember what we were talking about and that idea I had?" I can have an idea, tell him, and two months later it happens . . . or a month, three months, two days. It is that type of relationship and he is that type of a person; he listens to everything that I say.

When we first started doing this, Jim Frost drove me nuts. Calling me multiple times, twelve o'clock midnight, sound asleep, the phone would ring, and it was Jim. "Hey Todd, how are you doing? I hope I didn't wake you up?" And maybe he just wanted to know something: "Todd is that supposed to be black or blue?" Constantly thinking, that mind is constantly churning.

This was such a new business to him and he did what he had to do and he learned by asking. He is not too proud to ask somebody, and he surrounds himself with people that know what they are doing, in whatever facet of the business they are in.

It has been an unbelievable ride, teaming up with Jim. If we want to do something and we decide that we are going to do it, it gets done. I have absolutely no regret on anything we have done so far, I know anything we set to do we will accomplish it.

Frost is very superstitious. Don't do anything to jinx the shows. For example, we don't discuss with Frost an idea that we are going to try with an item, say a "Mystery Box" that we are going to run, as we did with the "Jeff Daniel's Mystery Box." We do not discuss how well the item is going to do. I don't say, "Jim, we are going to sell thousands." We don't jinx items like that.

Anything you are especially proud of?

When I air product, things come out of my mouth that I don't know that they are going to come out. For example, say that there is a bone handle and I started calling it "Antique Barn Board Jig." That is not the name on the box, its called "Peach Seed." I find other people starting to refer to it as whatever I said. I can change it and set a precedent on what things are called, way beyond my little group of people. Major companies that make knives will start referring to a particular item or handle material using the name that I made up. Like

Frost media crew poses for a group photo in the Cutlery Corner Network studio.

I said, it comes out; I don't put a thought into, "What am I going to call this?" It is a spur of the moment thing.

Some nights, like with Caribbean Blue bone, I have decided on the spur of the moment that I wanted a different name. Then over a two week period, I might end up calling the same knife handle three or four different names until I find one that comes out easier. I fool around with it and one will stick. Then I end up referring to it as that.

Have you ever heard the term "Ivorite?"

There is no such thing. [*Laughing*] I think Rex came up with that one. Now everybody calls it that. It is just white celluloid. I will watch the competition and they will call something a name and I know they watch my show. I know when they watch, because I hear what they say or how they refer to an item. It is not the correct name for it, so they had to watch my show.

CHAPTER 4

Frost Falcons Softball History
Building Character One Pitch at a Time

During my interview with Jeff Daniel, I asked him to fill me in on the history of softball and Frost Cutlery. Understandably, Jeff wanted to be sure to get all the facts and statistics correct on this topic, so instead of giving me this information orally, he graciously took the time to put it in writing. Accordingly, what follows is a brief overview of the involvement of Jim Frost and Frost Cutlery in the sport of women's fastpitch softball, and the accomplishments of the Frost Falcons teams, as recounted by Jeff.

JIM FROST HAS BEEN A PIONEER in bringing the sport of women's fastpitch softball to Tennessee. He has a genuine passion for kids, a desire to excel and a love for the game.

As Head Coach and Sponsor of the Frost Falcons softball teams from 1983 until 1993, Jim achieved an astonishing 527 wins and only 86 losses, for a .837 winning average. During this ten-year span, the Falcons were nationally ranked in the Top Ten in the Country.

When I think of what Mr. Frost has been able to accomplish as a coach and a sponsor, I can't help but think of some additional milestones that have impacted softball and our community. In 988, with the help of the City of Chattanooga and the Chattanooga Recreation Department, Mr. Frost and others were able to build a seven-field complex known as the Tyner Recreational Complex.

Thanks to Mr. Frost's influence and his drive to build that complex, literally thousands of kids have practiced and played on those fields each year. Not only was he busy building fields in 1988, he also hosted the Amateur Softball Association Nationals, which brought in fifty-five teams to Chattanooga from as far away as California.

During the next few years, from 1989 to approximately 1995, Mr.

Jim Frost Stadium, located in Warner Park, Chattanooga, Tennessee.

Frost began to sponsor the Frost Cutlery Collegiate Tournament. This tournament brought many top-ranked collegiate softball teams to Chattanooga, like Florida State, Louisiana Tech, North Carolina, South Carolina, Virginia, Nicholls State and many other great Universities and College teams.

In 1996, the Frost Falcons were granted an opportunity to play ainland China's Olympic fastpitch softball team in Columbus, Georgia, capping off a ten-year run that was nothing short of amazing.

Then in 1998 a truly world class softball stadium was built at Warner Park in Chattanooga. Spearheaded by Mr. Frost, with the help of many volunteers and much support from the community, the new stadium was named in Jim's honor. Today, the stadium is the home of the University of Tennessee-Chattanooga's nationally-ranked UTC Lady Mocs, and is open for regular play throughout the year. Some of the world's best players have played at Jim Frost Stadium.

Along with Jim's commitment to collegiate women's fastpitch softball, the entire Frost Cutlery family is justifiably proud of their own ASA team, the Frost Falcons. Following is a list of just some of the successes that the Frost Falcons have had in the Amateur Softball Association and other league[9] play from all age brackets:

1984 *Tennessee State Champions*

1985 *Tennessee State Champions*
South Atlantic Regional Champions

1986 *Tennessee State Runner-Up*

1987 *South Atlantic Regional Champions*

1988 *Tennessee State Champions*
South Atlantic Regional Champions
Junior Olympic Nationals
Nationals Runner-Up

1989 *Tennessee State Champions*
South Atlantic Regional Champions
Snyder/Oliver Champions

1990 *Tennessee State Champions*

---

9   The teams listed in this section compete in one of the following women's fastpitch softball leagues:

ASA	Amateur Softball Association
USFA	United States Fastpitch Association
NSA	National Softball Association
USSSA	United States Specialty Sports Association
NFA	North Florida Alliance
NASF	North American Sports Federation
SEAA	Sporting Events Association of America
NAFA	North American Fastpitch Association

1991 *Tennessee State Champions*
Tennessee State Runner-Up
South Atlantic Regional Champions

1992 *Tennessee State Champions*
South Atlantic Regional Champions

1993 *Tennessee State Runner-Up*

Even though Mr. Frost stopped coaching the team after 1993, the Frost Falcons have continued to be a fierce competitor around the nation. You will still find him at the ball fields, working with the kids or giving one of his famous motivational speeches.

But even without Jim's coaching, the Frost Falcons have continued on to further achievements. Here are some of many successes enjoyed by Frost Falcon teams from all age brackets:

1995 *North Carolina Classic Champions*

1997 *Tennessee State Champions*

1998 *District Champions*
Tennessee State Runner-Up
South Atlantic Region Runner-Up
World Qualifier Champions
Regional Qualifier Runner-Up

2003 *Fall Brawl Champions*
Summer Slam Champions
District Champions
Classic Champions

2004 *Fall Brawl Champions*

2005   *USSSA 8 & Under Champions*
USSSA 12 & Under Champions
March Blow Out Champions
Hot Shot Invitational – 1st Place
USSSA 8 & Under World Champions
USFA 8 & Under State Champions
NSA 8 & Under State Champions
SEAA 8 & Under State Champions
Franklin Frenzy 8 & Under Champions
GSA 8 & Under World Series Champions
March Madness 8 & Under – 1st Place
Rowdy Rumble Champions
NSA Hartselle Heat May Invitational – 1st Place
NSA One Day Champions
NASF Heritage Point – 1st Place
ASA Halloween Bash 12 & Under – 1st Place
NSA State Runner-Up
ASA 14 & Under Class A Runner-Up
USFA 14 & Under Paradise – 1st Place

2006   *USFA 12 & Under Border Battle – 1st Place*
Rossville Summer Blast – 3rd Place
USSSA 14 & Under State Champions
NSA Fastpitch Association Champions
Oktoberfest 8 & Under Tullahoma – 1st Place
ASA Lillian Edwards Memorial Tournament
USFA Alabama State Runner-Up
NAFA World Series Champions
NSA World Qualifier – 2nd Place
NSA World Qualifier – 1st Place

2007   *ASA 8 & Under National Invitation Champions*
USSSA 10 & Under World Qualifier Champions
NSA Early Bird Tournament Champions
World Series Warm-Up Runner-Up

8 & Under Rocket Springs Break Blast Champions
ASA 8& Under North Georgia Champions
USFA 10 & Under Class A World Champion
USFA 10 & Under State Champions
Classic 8 & Under Johnston Coca-Cola Champions
NSA 8 & Under Birmingham Memorial Champions
8 & Under Kentucky National Invitational Champs
USFA 8 & Under Regional Qualifier Runner-Up
USFA 8 & Under World Series – 2nd Place

2008 *NSA Scholarship Tournament Runner-Up*
USFA Summer Time Classic Champions
ASA 14 & Under Champions
Pro Fastpitch X-Treme Tour Champions

2009 *NSA State Champions*
NSA 16 & Under Division A World Series – 3rd Place
USFA 8 & Under World Series Champions
USFA 8 & Under Tennessee State Champions
ASA 8 & Under Make-A-Classic Champion
8 & Under Memorial Day Tournament Champion
8 & Under Powerhouse Payoff Tournament
ASA 8 & Under Diamond Classic Champions
Trussville Classic 8 & Under Champions

Jim has helped many high schools and universities with their softball programs but has done so anonymously in order to avoid bringing attention to himself. If you asked me to give you his biggest accomplishment in softball, I would have to say his joy comes from watching young players develop their potential and seeing over 200 student-athletes from the Falcon's organization receive scholarships to Colleges and Universities.

In recognition of his extraordinary commitment to the game and the young people who play it, Jim has received many awards and honors, including:

- Inducted into the ASA Hall of Fame
- Inducted into the Red Bank High School Hall of Fame on March 18, 2002
- Received the "Sandy" Sandlin Memorial Award on May 7, 1997
- Received the Chattanooga Area Old Timer's Association's "Man of the Year" Award for 1989-1990
- Inducted into the Chattanooga Sports Hall of Fame for his contributions, performance, character and integrity
- The Sporting Goods Manufacturers Association made Jim Frost its "Hero of the Year" for 1997
- The University of Tennessee at Chattanooga Entrepreneurial Hall of Fame Recipient 2011[1]

What more is there to say about a man that has given so much to fastpitch softball, physically, emotionally, and financially? You could press him about how much money he has given over the years, but the only reply you would get is a smile and, "It was for a good cause."

---

1   The statistics and achievements cited in this section were included to illustrate the decidedly beneficial affect that Jim Frost, the Frost Cutlery Company and its staff members have had on the world of fastpitch softball. They are only a partial list of the awards, accolades and championships that some of the in-house Frost Falcons softball teams have earned since their inception in 1983. Not included are the many achievements of all the other Frost Cutlery sponsored teams throughout the years.

    A prominent feature of Frost Cutlery's business office is a massive 72-foot-long trophy display case, but the company has never compiled an exact list of all its softball-related accomplishments. The research done by the company for this book covers the period from 1983 until 2009 and produced highlights from over 15,000 different softball games in which Frost Falcons teams competed. But there is much, much more, to be certain, and regrettably many noteworthy achievements did not make it into these pages.

Coach Jim Frost, Steve Frost and bat-girl little sister Stefanie Frost.

Coach Jim Frost and daughter Stefanie.

Pictured from left to right: Niece Kami Kelley, Coach Jim Frost, nephew Niles Kelley and daughter Stefanie, sporting some of the Frost Falcons uniforms.

Pictured from left to right: Daughter Stefanie Frost, Coach Jim Frost, niece Kami Kelley.

Coach Steve Frost and daughter Emerald.

Coach Jim Frost and daughter Stefanie.

Jim Frost surrounded by some of the trophies in the 72-foot trophy case at Frost Cutlery.

Future Hall of Famers? The Frost Falcon girls softball team who were the 2011 TSFA Fall World Series Champions clowns for the camera.

Jim and Jan Frost with former University of Tennessee head football coach Phil Fulmer.

Certificate recognizing Jim Frost as a Guest Coach for the University of Tennessee Lady Vols, with legendary head coach Pat Summitt, in a game against SEC rival Vanderbilt.

APPENDIX

To assist the reader, this Appendix contains a lexicon of terms used in this book, a list of Frost brand names, trade names, trademarks, definitions and letters from varied sources.

The Definitions section was added mostly because I always loved such sections in books that I have read, and it is basically a Jim Frost encyclopedia section. Hopefully it closes any loopholes that the reader may have after reading the other four chapters.

The section listing the various Frost Cutlery brand names, trade names and trademarks will assist the reader in possibly discovering that one of their favorite knife lines is really a Frost line.

The Letters section is a collection of just a few that Jim Frost and Frost Cutlery have received over the years. They speak for themselves.

Perhaps a few words about Frost Cutlery's partnerships and their endorsed lines of knives are also in order. The first of these partnerships started in 1987 with a handshake between Mr. James A. "Jim" Frost and Mr. Dale Earnhardt Sr. In the wake of that gentlemen's agreement, Frost Cutlery began making commemorative knives bearing the legendary Dale Earnhardt's name, likeness and autograph, and commemorating his many racing accomplishments. The relationship with Earnhardt naturally led to a partnership with Richard Childress (RCR) Racing, and both of these partnerships have made Frost Cutlery proud to be a supporter of NASCAR.

Frost Cutlery has also partnered with Mr. Bill Dance, host of Bill Dance Outdoors, and is happy to have carefully created a line of knives for the iconic Tennessee outdoorsman and sport fisherman.

One of Frost Cutlery's most creative partnerships has been with freelance knife and sword designer Russ Farrell. The Russ Farrell endorsed line of tactical folding knives and exquisite swords are museum pieces that are truly unique in their design and feel.

LEXICON

Bill Dance Outdoors — a popular cable television program hosted by well-known professional fisherman, Bill Dance. Frost Cutlery offers a line of Fishing & Outdoor knives endorsed by Dance.

Bolsters — Metal covers on both ends of a pocketknife usually made in nickel silver, brass or stainless steel. Bolsters can be polished smooth or engraved for decoration.

Bone — Used to make knife handles and scales, this source of this material is the shin bones of cattle from various countries of the world.

Bone coloring — Accomplished via a wipe on/wipe off process similar to wood staining, or by boiling bone in colored dyes for periods ranging from a few hours to a few weeks.

Buffalo horn — used to make knife handles and scales, the source of this material is derived from the horns of African Cape Buffalo.

Frost number — Frost Cutlery product identification number. The first two numbers or letters identify the country of manufacturer, as follows:

10	Taiwan	16/18	China
15	China	CW	Pakistan
17	Japan	HR	Germany
HK	China/Pakistan	35	35th Anniversary
OT	USA	40	40th Anniversary
14	Pakistan		

Corelon® — A Registered Trademark of Frost Cutlery, Corelon® knife handles and scales are handmade in the United States by artisans Michael Prater of Flintstone, Georgia, and Bud Hull of Rossville, Georgia, using a special acrylic polymer resin, and no two pieces are ever alike. Corelon® handles and scales are featured in many Frost Cutlery product lines, including Hen & Rooster and Case brand knives.

Dale Earnhardt, Inc. (DEI) — the company founded by the late, great NASCAR legend, Dale Earnhardt, who was also a close friend of Jim Frost. DEI is now owned by Earnhardt's widow, Teresa. Frost Cutlery's line of Earnhardt-endorsed Commemorative Knives are among the most collectible and valuable knives available today.

Deep etching — the process of using a strong acid and electricity to cut a design into the metal into a metal surface of the knife blade.

Frostwood® — A Registered Trademark for a laminated wood knife handle material developed and used by Frost Cutlery.

G-10 — a composite material made by baking compressed layers of fiberglass cloth soaked in resin. Because of its high strength, light weight, and because it is impervious to temperature changes, G-10 is commonly used in tactical folding knives.

Hen & Rooster® — This venerable German company has been manufacturing world renown cutlery in Solingen, Germany, since 1845 and is considered by many to be one of the greatest knife brands in the world. The company and the trademark have been owned by Frost Cutlery since 1983.

Jim Frost Stadium — Fastpitch softball stadium built in 1998 on the campus of the University of Tennessee-Chattanooga.

Larry Zehnder — Chattanooga Parks & Recreation Supervisor. Has worked closely with Jim Frost on many projects, including the Tyner ball fields and the Jim Frost Stadium.

Laser engraving — the process of using a computer-controlled laser to engrave or mark a knife blade, handle or wood presentation box.

Micarta — a composite of linen or paper fabric layers soaked in an epoxy resin and then cured. Micarta is incredibly lightweight and durable and thus an ideal material for making scales. Linen Micarta is the strongest and most popular.

Pad printing — A printing process that utilizes a computer and a special printer to transfer an image or logo onto a blade or handle.

Qualitas est familia institutio — Latin for "quality is a family tradition," this motto is laser engraved onto a blade of every Frost Family knife. Along with the Frost family crest, this motto also graces the cover of this book.

Ram or sheep horn — used to make knife handles and scales, this material is derived from the horns of rams and sheep indigenous to China.

Richard Childress Racing (RCR) — The NASCAR team owned by racing great and avid outdoorsman, Richard Childress. Frost Cutlery offers a line of RCR-endorsed Fishing & Hunting knife sets.

Rockwell hardness testing — consists of indenting the test material with a diamond cone or hardened steel ball indenter and measuring the depth of penetration. The blades of all Frost Cutlery Steel Warrior and Frost Family knives measure from 56 to 58 on the Rockwell HRC Scale.

Russ Farrell — Acclaimed designer, illustrator, product designer (*russfarrell.com*) and creator of the Designed by Russ Farrell line of knives and swords for Frost Cutlery.

Scales — two flat pieces of material that are attached to the flat sides of a folding blade knife or to the full tang of a fixed blade knife in order to form a handle.

Shield — a metal inlay featuring a trademark or logo or decoration that is inserted in the handle of a knife.

Stag horn — used to make knife handles and scales, this material is derived from the antlers of several deer species, including mule deer, whitetail deer, elk, red deer, Sambar stag and many others. Because deer naturally shed their antlers each season, deer stag horn is a sustainable and perpetually renewable material.

Tang stamp — normally located on the ricasso, which is the unsharpened area of the blade immediately adjacent to the guard or handle, the tang stamp bears the name and/or logo of the manufacturer of the knife, and may include other information, such as the product or serial number.

Women's fastpitch softball — A version of softball in which the pitcher throws the ball underhand at high speed after at least one windmill motion of the arm. Played on a smaller field than baseball with a larger ball, women's fastpitch softball is played nationwide and around the world at the Olympic, collegiate, high school and private youth league levels.

BRAND & TRADE NAMES

Barracuda®
Bear & Bull
Bear Hunter®
Beaver Creek
Black Hills Steel
Blade Master®
BuckCreek®
Buffalo Creek
Chef Deluxe®
Cherokee Cutlery
Chipaway®
Corelon®
Field Pro
Flying Falcon
Frost Cutlery®
Frost Family
Frost USA®
Hurricane®
Frostwood®
German Bull®
Hen & Rooster®
Master Angler®
Iron Horse®
Ocoee River Cutlery
Quick Silver
SilverHorse Stoneworks®
Steel Warrior®
Trophy Hunter
Trophy Stag
Uncle Lucky
Whitetail Cutlery

LETTERS & AWARDS

It is the feeling you get down deep inside—when you know you have contributed to mankind, when you know you have contributed to your community—that makes you think you've accomplished something truly worthwhile. — JIM FROST

Few people in the Tennessee Valley have ever done more for their community or for their neighbors than Jim Frost. While no good businessman is averse to good publicity, no decent human being is ever motivated to do a good thing simply because of the recognition and accolades he may garner in return. Jim Frost is both a decent human being and a great businessman who deserves to be lauded for his many selfless acts of care and kindness.

The letters reproduced on the following pages bear testament to Jim's kindness, his compassion, his generosity and his unabashedly philanthropic spirit, each of which virtues that, combined, have enabled Jim Frost to accomplish something truly worthwhile.

Jim Frost, with his mother, Margaret, and children, Stefanie and Stephen, receiving the 2008 Robert M. Artz Award presented by the National Recreation and Park Association.

National Recreation and Park Association

22377 Belmont Ridge Road
Ashburn, VA 20148-4501
703.858.0784
Fax 703.858.0794
www.nrpa.org

July 22, 2008

Dear Jim Frost,
6861 Mountain View Road
Ooltewah, TN 37363

I am very pleased to advise you of your selection as recipient of the NRPA Citizen Branch - ***Robert M. Artz Award*** for 2008.

We thank you for your participation during this year's program. Each year NRPA receives many fine candidates for this award program. This year your selection was made from an impressive field of candidates.

The formal presentation of this award will be held during the Citizen Branch awards reception, at our Congress and Exposition at Baltimore, Maryland, which will be held at 6:00 – 7:30 pm on Thursday, October 16, 2007.

Please confirm with me at 703-858-2190, that you will be attending this event. Additionally, I will need some brief biographical information from you (Less than 200 words), as well as a black & white photograph. Please send this information to moriley@nrpa.org.

On behalf of the National Recreation and Park Association, please accept my congratulations for this most prestigious recognition.

Sincerely,

Marianne O'Riley
NRPA Award Programs Manager

City of Chattanooga
DEPARTMENT OF PARKS & RECREATION
1102 South Watkins Street
Chattanooga, Tennessee 37404

January 3, 2008

Mr. Jim Frost
Frost Cutlery
6861 Mountain View road
Ooltewah, Tennessee 37363

Dear Jim:

First of all I want to thank you for your genuine commitment to helping the youth of our community develop their God given talents. I really appreciate your commitment to the Warner Park Project and the construction of the restroom/concession building as designed. The project will be a tremendous new addition to our park system.

Also, your contribution of commemorative gifts for our sister city officials in Wuxi, China were greatly appreciated. I had the enclosed picture developed and framed for you which shows our gifts being opened by the most important official in the Wuxi City government, Yu Shun Yuan and the Director of Foreign Affairs, Zhao Ming. Wuxi's population will soon surpass five million people and has been a sister city partner of Chattanooga for twenty five years, one of the oldest relationships between China and the United States.

We thank you for producing this commemorative knife for this China event. It brought many smiles and fortified an even stronger relationship.

Before closing, I also want to take this opportunity to thank you for the beautiful 35 year commemorative knife display presented by Santa McDonald. It is being proudly displayed in my office and is such a beautiful presentation of the quality of your products.

I wish you the very best for a prosperous New Year. Thanks for everything you do to support our City.

Sincerely,

Lawrence A. Zehnder CPRP
Administrator
Chattanooga Parks & Recreation

LAZ/we

cc: Mayor Ron Littlefield

City of Chattanooga
Office of the Mayor

Proclamation

WHEREAS: Jim Frost was recognized in October of 2008 by the 7,000 member National Recreation and Park Association, the United States' leading advocate for Parks and Recreation Programming, for his volunteer and advocacy contributions to the Chattanooga Community, and

WHEREAS: Jim successfully took on the development of a world class women's fast pitch softball stadium for the youth of the community by raising all the necessary funds and donations to build the Chattanooga "Field of Dreams," and

WHEREAS: Jim's desire to show his continuing support for the youth of the community and those throughout the country who visit Warner Park by contributing all funds and donations necessary to build the "Snooks Nerron" facility which is now the centerpiece of the $4 million dollar Warner Park Development accomplished in the summer of 2008, and

WHEREAS: Jim has gained recognition world-wide, in support of his community and the Sister Cities Program, by creating a one-of-a-kind memento presented to the Mayor of Wuxi, China, a community of over five million citizens during a Friendship Summit in October of 2007

NOW, THEREFORE, I, Ron Littlefield, Mayor of the
City of Chattanooga, do hereby wish to honor and recognize the efforts of

Mr. Jim Frost

For his dedicated and tireless commitment to the City of Chattanooga, the Parks and Recreation Department, and the advancement of one of our community's greatest pastimes, Softball.

In Witness Whereof, I have hereunto set my hand and caused the
Seal of the City of Chattanooga to be affixed this the
1st day of September, 2009

Ron Littlefield, Mayor

City of Chattanooga
DEPARTMENT OF PARKS & RECREATION

September 16, 2009

Ozark Small Press

Attention: Scott Cuffe

On behalf of the City of Chattanooga Department of Parks and Recreation, I want to personally acknowledge the tremendous contributions Jim Frost has made in advancing, not only the quality of sports facilities in Chattanooga, but also the continuing attention given to our aspiring young athletes.

Jim has assisted the City in creating one of the country's top stadiums for young athletes which has become the envy of thousands of visiting participants. The coordinated effort he was able to bring about among business and sports enthusiasts to create this fabulous venue was exceptional. He was able to instill a contagious dream giving the community a desire to provide the best possible facility where dreams for college careers can be realized.

The Field of 1000 Dreams was realized and hundreds of our youth have been inspired to set goals and achieve their aspirations. The development of quality facilities communicates the level of importance this community places on providing constructive and beneficial alternatives to the temptations engulfing the youth of our community.

Mr. Frost's effort to improve Chattanooga youth sports facilities may have started with Frost Stadium but it continues to this day. The youth facilities at the Tyner Recreation Center received the attention of Jim's improvement efforts in 2005-2006. The non-profit youth association experienced new restrooms, lighting, parking lot and many other improvements as a result of Jim's ability to influence people who can make a difference.

The redevelopment of Warner Park into a specialized youth athletic venue had Jim's involvement from the very beginning. His contributions in developing the complex's main support building provides the complex cornerstone from which the new fields emanate. Within twelve months of the Warner Park Development, Jim's support and influence was seen in the opening of the award winning Summit of Softball Complex. This twelve million dollar facility came about due to the support of elected officials but the community had the opportunity of a clearer vision due to the accomplishments of prior years provided by Jim and his unselfish efforts toward the development of quality facilities. The dream originally articulated by Jim Frost in setting the course for the softball stadium is still being realized in each new sports facility the City of Chattanooga initiates.

Chattanooga has experienced a re-birth in the last twenty years that the world has noticed. Citizens in the community have made this possible through their leadership, vision and private contributions leading the way. Parks and Recreation's advancement is a significant part of this re-birth adding amenities which provide the quality of life experienced by our visitors and citizens. Jim Frost's involvement and contributions in our parks and facility development is a contributing factor to Chattanooga's re-birth. His many hours of involvement have truly helped to revitalize a community, making not only dreams of our youth come true but those of all the citizens of Chattanooga.

We congratulate him on his successes and look forward to working with him on his next effort to serve the young people of our community!

Sincerely,

Lawrence A. Zehnder, CPRP
Administrator

LAZ/we

The University of Tennessee, Softball Office, 117 Stokely Athletics Center, Knoxville, TN 37996-3110　　865-974-4275 (Phone)　　865-974-8914 (Fax)

utladyvols.com

TO: Mr. Scott Cuffe
　　　Ozark Small Press

RE: Mr Jim Frost

Date: 20 Sep 09

Dear Mr. Cuffe,

Jim Frost is a special man who has spent his life helping others succeed. He is directly responsible for giving numerous young women the means and facilities to perfect their softball skills. As a coach and mentor, he directly influences these athletes to be better students and better citizens. His support of our game has enabled countless young athletes to receive college scholarships. The life lessons he and his coaches teach prepare them for college and life afterwards.

Jim is unselfish and does not seek publicity for his deeds. His satisfaction comes from seeing athletes from his programs graduate from college and become responsible citizens in their communities.

Karen and I first met Jim a few days after we arrived in Chattanooga to coach the University of Tennessee-Chattanooga (UTC) softball program. The team was in last place in the conference and had no assigned field for practice and games. They were playing on a city park field that they shared with recreational teams. Jim, who was already nationally known as a youth softball coach, told Karen and I that he was going to do everything he could to help us become more competitive. He felt that by upgrading the local college program, he could also further promote the sport with the youth of the community. That same day, he told us that his goal was to help every young player in the city have an opportunity to follow their dreams and compete for college scholarships. Jim gathered other sponsors and augmented our funding to a new level. We won a share of the conference crown our first year. At the start of our second season, he told our players he was going to build them "the finest softball stadium in the country." His dream was to make the stadium a showcase for UTC, and also a place that all the youth in the community could share.

The rest is history. Jim spearheaded the drive to build the "Stadium of 1000 Dreams." He has also been an integral part of upgrading two separate softball facilities in Chattanooga. UTC has become the dominant team in the Southern Conference, and many, many young athletes receive scholarship offers from numerous college coaches who now make the city a regular stop on their recruiting calendars. Jim was essential in bringing the first ever USA Olympic Team to Chattanooga in 1996, and that exhibition game energized the community to get behind Jim in his quest to build the stadium that would eventually bear his name. Their appearance motivated thousands of other youth to play the game Jim Frost loves.

When Karen and I moved to the University of Tennessee Knoxville campus, Jim continued to support our Program as well as many others. Jim has accompanied our University of Tennessee team to the Women's College World Series on three occasions and has proudly observed several of "his girls" play in the prestigious Southeastern Conference.

Karen and I love Jim Frost. He is first and foremost a mentor whose counsel we value. He knows more about softball than most coaches I have met. He is a proud, compassionate person who cares deeply about his fellow man. He walks his talk. Perhaps most importantly, he is a true friend.

Sincerely,

Ralph Weekly

Ralph Weekly
Co-Head Coach, University of Tennessee
USA Olympic Coach and Staff Member
1996 and 2000

DEPARTMENT OF THE ARMY
HSC, DIVISION SPECIAL TROOPS BATTALION
CAMP VICTORY, IRAQ
APO AE 09342

REPLY TO
ATTENTION OF:

AFDR-SAA-CHJ

20 DEC 2008

MEMORANDUM FOR RECORD

TO: MR. JIM FROST / FROST CUTLERY

SUBJECT: CHRISTMAS GIFT

1. The purpose of this letter is to offer a word of gratitude for the gift extended by Mr. Jim Frost and the employees of FROST CUTLERY. Mere words will not adequately express the thanks your organization deserves for supporting Soldiers engaged in OPERATION IRAQI FREEDOM.

2. This letter cannot overstate the impact your mission had on the well-being of Soldiers and in turn how this effects how they fight the Global War on Terrorism. I have watched troops on numerous occasions open packages and it never gets old. The expressions on their faces and the emotions exhibited are priceless as they receive care packages and goodies from strangers. The pocket knives from Mr. Jim Frost and FROST CUTLERY were no exception. It generated enthusiasm and appreciation to all Soldiers receiving your gift. Though you may not be able to wear a uniform or travel to distant lands, you are a vital part of serving our great nation through this current conflict.

3. Further, and on a personal note, when I opened the package and read the accompanying letter it took me back to my adolescence. One of my first pocket knives was a PARKER-FROST bone-handled, lock blade knife that I carried as a young boy. Thank you for taking me back to those days and for your gift. I will treasure it for many years.

4. Enclosed you will find a small token of appreciation from the Soldiers of the 10th Mountain Division – Light Infantry. As the certificate states, this flag was flown over our Corps Headquarters on the stated date. It is noteworthy to mention that the picture in the background is one of Saddam Hussein's former palaces and houses our Corp Headquarters.

5. Point of Contact for this memorandum is undersigned at:

CH(CPT) Michael D. Jones

MICHAEL D. JONES
CHAPLAIN, CPT
10TH MTN DIV (LI)
CAMP VICTORY, IRAQ

ENTREPRENEURSHIP
HALL *of* FAME
THE
UNIVERSITY*of*TENNESSEE*at*CHATTANOOGA **Uf**
COLLEGE *of* BUSINESS

TWO THOUSAND AND ELEVEN INDUCTEES

JAMES A FROST

Jim Frost began his career humbly, as a modest, everyday shift worker at a chemical plant, collecting pocket knives. He never dreamed of turning his hobby of collecting and trading knives into a multi-million dollar family business.

As a hardworking laborer, Mr. Frost used his drive for success to create a new company, selling knives in his lunch bucket. From 1969 to 1978, Jim saw his business interest in knives grow with the formation of the Frost Distributing company in 1972 and then with the importation of cutlery under the Frost Cutlery® tang stamp in 1978. Frost's labor of love has grown to encompass over 25 of its own world renowned product-lines. This Frost family of brands includes such trademarks as Hen & Rooster®, German Bull™, and Steel Warrior® knives. Frost Cutlery is now headquartered in a 150,000 square foot warehouse in Ooltewah, TN, with over 150 associates.

As owner of Frost Cutlery, Jim not only became a sophisticated businessman and successful entrepreneur, but also developed a heartfelt compassion for philanthropy. Utilization of the success of his cutlery business to help others, exemplifies Mr. Frost's passion & desire to give back for the betterment of the community. His investment in the lives of young student athletes and his community resulted in the creation of a foundation, which will continue his legacy.

Mr. Frost's love for the game of softball was inevitable after coaching and sponsoring his own daughter's Frost Falcon's softball team. He was the visionary and organizer for the construction of a 7-field sports facility known as Tyner Recreation Complex, underwrote and sponsored Frost Cutlery Collegiate Tournaments, and in 1998 spearheaded a world class softball facility, Jim Frost Stadium, at Warner Park — now home to the University of Tennessee at Chattanooga Lady Mocs.

Jim Frost's inspiration comes from watching the youth of our community develop their potential both on and off the field. He has helped over 200 student athletes receive college scholarships. Jim Frost believes, "Those who seek, listen, learn, and utilize the intelligence of others are the wisest people in the world. We are given just one life to live and what we choose to do with it is up to us. Some may choose to waste it away, but many will choose to follow their dreams and ambitions." Jim Frost pursued his American dream, starting with a lunch bucket and a vision, but the best chapter of his legacy has yet to be written.

In 2011, Jim Frost was honored to be inducted into the University of Tennessee at Chattanooga's College of Business Entrepreneurship Hall of Fame.

AFTERWORD

T HE FROST LEGACY will endure for many generations to come, well beyond Jim Frost's lifetime and well beyond the lifetimes of his children and their children's children. And just as with all other legacies, the vast majority of the lives that have been touched by Mr. Frost's own legacy will never be known to him.

So what if? What if a shiftworker named Jim Frost had decided not to step away from his modest job at a local chemical plant and start Frost Cutlery Company? Would his life have had the same impact on those around him and on his community?

The answer, of course, can never be truly known. But almost certainly there would be no Frost Stadium and no Frost Falcons scholarship program. Nowhere near as many deserving young girls would be attending college on softball scholarships. Chattanooga, Tennessee would likely not be renowned for women's fastpitch softball, and national softball tournaments most likely wouldn't be coming to the city, helping to drive its tourism-based economy.

With no Frost Cutlery Company there would be no Frost Masonic knives for Grand Master Ed Jennings to sell for the benefit of the children's home in Macon, Georgia. There would be one less leading community leader for Chattanooga to look to for inspiration and philanthropic endeavors. There would be fewer beds at T. C. Thompson Children's Hospital and many sick children would be forced to go elsewhere or turned away for treatment. Much like a scene from the beloved movie *It's a Wonderful Life*, the city of Chattanooga and its community would be dramatically different if there was no Jim Frost.

But, happily, that's not what happened.

Instead, Jim Frost did what came to him naturally. He took a risk, stepped out on his own and moved forward toward his goals with a passion fueled by doing what he loved doing the most. As he bettered himself, he made sure that those around him were bettered as well. As his prosperity grew, so did his giving. He surrounded himself with good, hardworking people, into whom he poured all the best qualities of himself. Together they built one of the largest, longest lasting cutlery companies that this country has ever seen.

More important, Jim Frost built a legacy that will provide a lasting benefit for generations to come. From future Frost Cutlery employees, to players on Frost Falcons softball teams yet to be formed, to all the children—many as yet unborn—who will be saved or healed as the result of the care they will someday receive at T. C. Thompson Children's Hospital, the ripple effect of Mr. Frost's giving ways will touch the lives of untold numbers of people for decades to come.

You, dear reader, are invited to share in and be a part of that legacy. While you may never know Jim Frost personally or be an employee of Frost Cutlery company or even own a Frost Cutlery knife, as long as you instill in yourself the indomitable "yes I can" spirit that Jim Frost has long striven to impart to all around him, you will not only keep that spirit alive but also make it your own.

That is the Jim Frost legacy that will endure forever.

A NOTE FROM THE AUTHOR

After 20 years as a police officer in Arizona, I retired to the Ozarks in southwest Missouri. Paradise found. My first book, *Arizona Cop Stories*, was released in December of 2008.

I contemplated some of my favorite things and decided on my next book, *Frost Cutlery: History & Tribute*. I wrote a letter to Frost Cutlery and asked them to give me unprecedented access to their world so that I could write their story. That letter, along with a picture of me and my beloved black Lab, Ellee, led to a phone call with the company's senior vice president, Jeff Daniel, who graciously green-lighted my trip to Frost Cutlery's Tennessee headquarters and to the studio where the *Cutlery Corner Network* television show was produced at that time.

After conducting more than twenty separate interviews with the family, friends and staff of Mr. James A. "Jim" Frost during a visit to the Frost Cutlery headquarters in August 2009, and later, after many more telephone interviews and e-mails, I sat down to write this book. I did not want this story to be a simple retelling of everyone's stories in my words. Therefore, I made the decision to let them all relate the story of Jim Frost and the Frost Cutlery Company in their own words.

This book is a history lesson for us all and, even more, a tribute to a great American man and his company, proving that with hard work, perseverance, and love, the American Dream does come true.

Scott Cuffe
www.ozarksmallpress.com